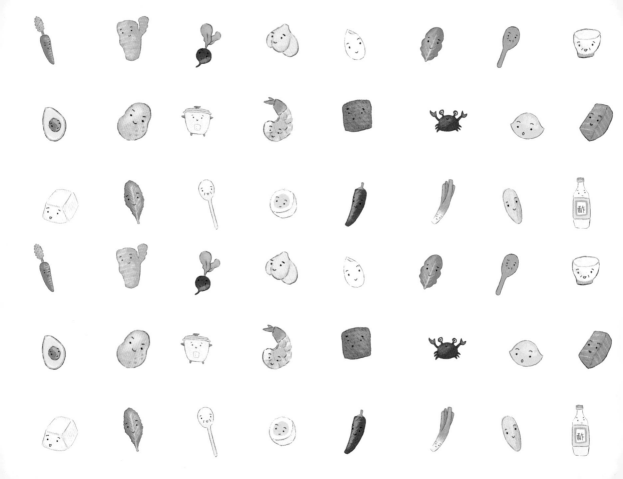

RICE CRAFT

YUMMY! **HEALTHY!** FUN TO MAKE!

Sonoko Sakai

photographs by **Matt Armendariz**

CHRONICLE BOOKS
SAN FRANCISCO

Library of Congress Cataloging-in-Publication Data available.
ISBN 978-1-4521-4287-6

Manufactured in China

MIX
Paper from
responsible sources
FSC® C008047

Designed by VANESSA DINA
Food styling by SONOKO SAKAI
Typesetting by FRANK BRAYTON

Chronicle books and gifts are available at special quantity
discounts to corporations, professional associations, literacy
programs, and other organizations. For details and discount
information, please contact our premiums department at
corporatesales@chroniclebooks.com or at 1-800-759-0190.

10 9 8 7 6 5 4 3 2 1

Chronicle Books LLC
680 Second Street
San Francisco, California 94107
WWW.CHRONICLEBOOKS.COM

To my family and extended family,
near and far, especially the young
ones—Mai, Masa, Mako, Miki,
Hayato, Sofia, and Paolo.

INTRODUCTION:
RICE RITUALS

Every onigiri has a story. My story takes me back to the 1960s, when I was growing up in Kamakura in Kanagawa Prefecture, not far from Tokyo. Down the street from where we lived, a small family owned a rice mill, where the townspeople bought freshly milled rice. The pleasant nutty aroma of the rice bran always permeated the shop. One of the old miller's morning rituals was to write a haiku on the blackboard that hung outside his business, such as this famous one by Basho:

Old pond
Frog jumped in
Sound of water

The seasonal verses entertained the passersby, including the tourists who came to visit Daibutsu, the Big Buddha of Kamakura. Sometimes the miller wrote children's verses for us to sing out loud. My mother always praised his calligraphy, and on occasion she asked him to write letters for her.

In the late spring, as I rode the train to school, I could glimpse the farmers in the rice paddies, planting seedlings by hand. When

the days got warmer, the rice stalks grew and turned into a lush green carpet, thriving with life—tadpoles, nymphs, dojo loach, and water striders. The most exciting time was during the fall harvest, when the farmers cut the golden rice stalks and hung them on wooden racks to dry in the sun. Their work never seemed to end.

The wife of one of the farmers visited our house regularly, carrying a huge bamboo basket—a portable vegetable shop—on her back. Daikon radishes, kabocha squash, eggplants, cucumbers, and delicate offerings of fermented soybeans wrapped in rice husks and farm eggs wrapped in old newspapers. Whatever she pulled out of that basket amazed us kids. Her basket became particularly heavy after the rice harvest, because she was carrying "new crop" rice. New crop rice tastes delicious, because it's so fresh. Though I was not a child of a rice miller or a rice farmer, one of the Japanese rituals of growing up was to pray for a good rice harvest. I still do.

My favorite way to eat rice is to make onigiri. My grandmother's onigiri were divine. She made rice in a small cast-iron pot on the wood-burning stove in the living room. She lived next door to us, so I would visit her every day, and she would often treat me to onigiri. I enjoyed the time we passed together while we waited for the rice to cook. She told me stories of her girlhood, of her favorite scenes in *The Merchant of Venice* and *Romeo and Juliet*, of the Chaliapin steak—named for the famous Russian opera singer who visited Japan in 1908—her

parents had treated her to when she was a young girl. Japanese people hardly ate beef back then, so eating that piece of meat was a cultural awakening for my grandmother.

When the rice was cooked and we opened the lid, the steam would rise and fog up my grandmother's glasses. Seconds later, a grassy aroma would fill the room. Grandmother would give the rice a quick turn with her wooden rice paddle and make the onigiri while the rice was still warm. Her onigiri were filled with *okaka*

(hand-shaved bonito flakes seasoned with a few drops of soy sauce) and wrapped in crispy *nori* (dried seaweed). We would sit on the sunny porch with a view of her garden, eating the onigiri. The first bite smelled of Kamakura's salty sea breeze. The second bite was full of the taste of the delicately sweet and tender rice, and the third bite of the smoky okaka. I never wanted these delicious times to end.

It is now my turn to share my love for rice and onigiri with you. For most of my adult life, I have made Los Angeles my home with my husband, Katsunisa, and our son, Sakae. During the summer holidays, Tyler, my stepson, came to visit us from London. I was always busy feeding the boys. Crispy grilled onigiri was their favorite food on the BBQ. Since the 1980s, I have been teaching Japanese cooking classes and writing about food. My first cookbook, *The Poetical Pursuit of Food: Japanese Recipes for American Cooks*, was a collection of stories and recipes about the days spent in the kitchens of my mother and grandmother, as well as my own in California. My cooking philosophy has remained the same: freshness, beauty, simplicity, health, and fun are what matter most to me in the kitchen.

In 2011, I started a project called Common Grains, dedicated to sharing the Japanese tradition and pleasures of eating grains and vegetables as part of a healthy lifestyle. I have gone back to Japan every year to visit and learn from farmers and artisans, sake brewers, katsuobushi makers, and miso makers, and to study noodle making by hand. With a generous seed grant from Glenn Roberts of Anson Mills, I have also been working with Southern California farmers, bakers, chefs, and cooks to restore the Southern California grain hub that existed until the beginning of the twentieth century. Our goal is to reestablish such heirloom wheats as Sonora White, emmer, and Red Fife, and other grains like barley, buckwheat, rye, and oats, and to advocate for sustainable agriculture and the value of food grown close to home.

Rice has been particularly important to me, as it

forms the foundation of my Japanese heritage. With my collaborators, I have made thousands of onigiri at pop-up dinners, contests, food trucks, and workshops in California, Washington, Hawaii, and Hong Kong. I hosted the Rice Fest in Honolulu, where our onigiri contestants made the biggest Spam musubi in the world!

I am inspired by the outpouring of love for onigiri I encounter everywhere. The onigiri gatherings bring together formalists, who lean toward traditional Japanese shapes and fillings, and freestylers, who throw tradition out the door. No matter which camp people belong to, onigiri promote community and appreciation for food made by hand.

This book is a blend of tradition and originality. You will find classic onigiri (plain rice, a filling, and a dab of sea salt, wrapped in a piece of crispy nori) and creative onigiri (of the sort that shine at my pop-ups and workshops). My hope is to share a little taste of Japan and of my cooking philosophy, and a lot of flavor and fun with you. I hope to hear your onigiri story in person someday.

CHAPTER ONE:
ONIGIRI FUNDAMENTALS
AND MASTER RECIPES

Making onigiri is simple. They are rice shaped by hand into a ball, filled with a bit of savory something, and often finished off with a wrap of nori. Onigiri are similar to nigiri sushi; in fact, both *nigiri* and *onigiri* mean the same thing: "to mold." Broadly speaking, sushi is rice seasoned with vinegar and salt and topped with a piece of fish. Onigiri is made with a greater emphasis on the rice. Think of a burrito, but daintier, with surprises inside and out. Sushi is prepared by a chef; onigiri is made by moms. Onigiri is both a comfort food and the darling of convenience stores. I don't know of another snack that enjoys this dual status.

Another popular way to label onigiri is *omusubi*, which means "to form as a whole." In this book, I will use only the term *onigiri*.

Onigiri comes in infinite flavor combinations and shapes. The recipes I offer include Japanese classics, passed down from my mother and grandmother, as well as modern creations from my California kitchen and playful innovations inspired by the onigiri shops in Japan. Once you learn the technique, you'll soon be inventing your own delicious onigiri.

RICE

Use sticky rice to make onigiri. Also known as sushi rice, varieties include short-grain Japonica and Japanese-style medium-grain rice. These varieties cling together when cooked and hold their shape when molded. They are available in Asian markets, natural food stores, some supermarkets, and online. Long-grain varieties like jasmine and basmati are not used for making onigiri, because they are not sticky enough to form a cohesive mass, but they can be blended in small amounts with short- or medium-grain rice. (See Adding Whole Grains and Beans to Rice on page 22).

WHITE RICE

When brown rice is milled, the bran and germ are polished away. The starchy endosperm that's left is white rice. It's carb heaven. White rice is enjoyed for its mild sweetness, subtle aroma, translucency, and tender texture. White rice is not very nutritious when you compare it to brown rice, but it's easier to digest, more versatile, and cooks in half the time.

Short-Grain Japonica Rice

Japonica rice has been a staple in Japan since ancient times. It's a tender, viscous, and sticky rice. Among the hundreds of distinct varieties of Japanese rice, Koshihikari and Akitakomachi are two of the most popular, and are widely grown in California. These varieties taste good even at room temperature, which make them ideal for onigiri. The flavors and textures of Japonica are said to vary, depending on where and how the rice is grown, akin to the terroir of wine.

Japanese-Style Medium-Grain Rice

There are several varieties of medium-grain rice grown in California that contain the sticky trait of Japonica rice that is so good for making onigiri. Heirloom Kokuho Rose, developed and grown by Koda Farms, the oldest rice farm in Dos Palos, California, was bred to suit that locality's microclimate and soil type. The rice is tender in texture and subtly sweet, with a nuanced floral bouquet. My mother used to take this rice back to Japan as *omiyage* (souvenirs). There is also medium-grain Calrose rice available.

Sweet Rice

Sweet rice is another Japonica cultivar. It is glutinous rice used primarily for making pounded rice cakes called mochi. The grains are clingy and result in a comforting sticky texture the Japanese are obsessed with and use the term *mochi mochi* to describe. (I even like my bread and pastries to be mochi mochi.) You can add 1 to 2 Tbsp of sweet rice or sweet brown rice into your rice mixture to achieve this texture. (See Adding Whole Grains and Beans to Rice, page 22).

BROWN RICE

Brown rice is unmilled rice in its whole-grain form. The husk is removed from the kernel to reveal the brown grain. Rich in dietary fiber and vitamins B and E, brown rice also contains beneficial oils. It has an umami-rich, grassy flavor and a nutty aroma. Brown rice needs to soak for a few hours, or overnight, before cooking and takes longer to cook, and even chew, than white rice, but if you are looking for nutrition, brown rice is the way to go.

Haiga Rice or Haigamai

Haiga rice takes its name from the Japanese word for "germ." It's brown rice that has been "semi-milled," meaning that some of the bran is polished away but the germ remains intact. The germ retains the oils; some of the fiber; vitamins B1, B2, B6, E; and GABA (gamma butyric acid). Haiga rice was popularized in the 1920s in

Japan to combat beriberi, a disease caused by vitamin B1 (thiamine) deficiency. Haiga rice is beige in color, and has a slight nutty flavor and a tender texture. This rice cooks in the same amount of time and with the same rice-to-water ratio as white rice, making it easier to use than brown rice and easier to digest.

Sprouted Brown Rice

This is a germinated brown rice, also sold as GABA rice by some rice producers. The germination process adds a ton of nutrients by waking up the dormant enzymes such as gamma-aminobutryic acid (GABA). Sprouting also softens the outer bran layer of the rice kernel, making it more digestible than regular brown rice. Eating sprouted brown rice is said to lower anxiety and blood pressure and improve cardiovascular functions.

It is easy to make sprouted brown rice at home. The ideal temperature for sprouting is between 84° and 104°F [30° and 40°C]. It takes about 2 days for the rice to sprout. To make 5 cups [600 g] of cooked sprouted brown rice, measure 1½ cups [300 g] of brown rice and put it in a bowl. Cover with 3 cups [720 ml] lukewarm water and let soak for 8 hours. After 8 hours of soaking, rinse and drain completely. Repeat rinsing and draining, two or three times a day every 4 to 6 hours. Rinsing helps remove the funky smell that is formed by the beneficial bacteria. You will notice that the tip of each grain of rice will become fuller and larger as the rice germinates. Tiny white buds less than $\frac{1}{16}$ in [2 mm] long will sprout. At this point, sprouting is complete. Rinse the rice and drain the soaking water completely. Don't let the rice sprout any further, because it won't taste good. Sprouted brown rice requires less water to cook than regular brown rice does. Just add 1¾ cups [420 ml] of filtered water and cook as you would white rice (see page 18). The drained sprouted rice can be covered and stored in the fridge for 2 days.

STORING RICE

Freshly milled "new crop" white rice is highly sought after by Japanese consumers for its good fragrance and flavor. In fact, in Japan, the milling date is required by law to appear on the rice package. (This isn't required in the United States.) White rice tastes best within one month of its milling date during the summer and three months during the winter. As rice gets older, it oxidizes and the flavor deteriorates. A year after harvest, rice is classified as *komai* (mold rice), which still has a shelf life of another year or two, as long as it is properly stored in a dark, cool place with a tight-fitting lid. Store brown rice in the fridge or freezer because the bran layer is more likely to go rancid than white rice.

When using older white rice, soak it in water overnight. To improve the flavor of older rice, blend it with an equal amount of new crop rice. You can also add 2 to 3 Tbsp of sweet rice to give it some oomph.

RICE COOKERS AND POTS

Those of us who eat rice on a regular basis have a few theories about how to make the best rice. I go back and forth between cooking rice on the stove top and using an electric rice cooker.

The stove-top method is the classic way to cook rice, using a cast-iron, heavy-bottomed pot with a tight-fitting lid. I use a Le Creuset or Lodge Dutch oven with a capacity of 2 to 3 qt [2 to 2.8 L], depending on how much rice I plan to cook. Be sure to select a pot that's deep enough to allow for the rice to expand to about three times its original size. The Japanese donabe rice cooker makes heavenly rice, with grains that stand up when cooked. I have a Kamado-san donabe rice cooker that retains heat nicely and is easy to use. The pressure cooker, though it can be a little intimidating, is also excellent for cooking brown rice, because there is no need to soak the brown rice and it cooks faster than any other method. Brown rice cooked in a pressure cooker tastes nutty, with a stickiness that is addictive.

The electric rice cooker is both reliable and indispensable for people who eat large quantities of rice. I use my rice cooker as much as I use my toaster. I have a Tiger rice cooker that comes with all the bells and whistles; it makes plain rice in different textures and varieties (for example, short-grain white rice, short-grain brown rice, and long-grain rice), cooks mixed grains and oatmeal, and has a fermentation button for making bread, though I have never used that. Even the simplest rice cooker, with just an on-and-off button, can do marvels with rice.

When my son, Sakae, went away for college, I sent him off with a 10-lb [4.5-kg] bag of rice and a rice cooker. He often made a quick meal of rice with some kind of meat protein. I was astounded when I found a box full of

Spam stashed away under the bed in his dorm room. It turns out he was making Spam *musubi*, which I discovered is a very popular onigiri in Hawaii.

HOW TO COOK RICE FOR ONIGIRI

Rice for making onigiri should be fully cooked and slightly firm to the bite, like sushi rice from a good sushi maker, though some people prefer a softer texture for their onigiri. You be the judge. Use the water-to-rice ratio in the recipes as a guide, because different rice varieties cook at different water-to-rice ratios depending on the age of the rice, the quality of the water (for example, soft or hard water), and altitude. High altitude will affect cooked rice differently, so the best thing to do is cook a few test batches with smaller amounts of rice to figure out how to get desirable texture first.

Rinsing rice washes away nutrients (bran), so give the grains just a light rinse, using your cupped hand to gently swish the grains for about 10 seconds to clean the rice. Avoid rinsing for longer than that because it will crack the grains and make the cooked rice mushy. There is also white rice sold as *musenmai*, or "no-rinse rice."

WHITE RICE
ᴼᴿ HAIGA RICE

To cook basic white rice and haiga rice, I measure enough water to equal 110 to 120 percent of the volume of uncooked rice. It's important that you read the instructions on the rice package to see what water-to-rice ratio the producer recommends. The amount of water depends on the altitude, the variety and freshness of the rice, and how firm or soft you want the cooked rice to be. The fresher the rice, the less water you need. For new crop white rice, use equal amounts of water and uncooked rice. Combine the rice and water and let soak for about 30 minutes in the summertime and 1 hour during the wintertime. If using an electric rice cooker, pressure cooker, or donabe, follow the manufacturer's instructions.

1½ cups [300 g] medium- or short-grain white rice or haiga rice

1¾ cups [420 ml] filtered water

½ tsp sea salt (optional)

Place the rice in a medium bowl and rinse under cool running water, using your hands to gently swish the grains for about 10 seconds. Drain completely.

Pour the filtered water into a heavy-bottomed pot with a tight-fitting lid. Add the rice and salt (if using) and let soak for 30 minutes, or overnight.

Place the pot, uncovered, over medium heat and bring to a boil. The water should bubble around the rim evenly. Cover the pot, turn the heat to very low, and cook, without peeking, for 20 minutes. Remove from the heat and, without opening the lid, let stand for 15 minutes.

Uncover the pot and gently fluff the rice with a rice paddle or wooden spoon. Re-cover and let stand for 5 minutes more. When cool enough to handle, the rice is ready to make onigiri; use immediately.

MAKES ABOUT 5 CUPS [600 G]

BROWN RICE

When cooking brown rice, it is important that you read the instructions on the rice package to see what water-to-rice ratio the producer recommends, because short-grain brown rice, medium-grain brown rice, and sprouted brown rice cook at different ratios. To cook short-grain brown rice, I measure enough water to equal about 180 percent of the volume of the uncooked rice. Be sure to soak your brown rice in the water overnight. If using an electric rice cooker, pressure cooker, or donabe, follow the manufacturer's instructions. The salt helps the rice absorb the water and adds flavor.

1½ cups [300 g] short-grain brown rice

2¾ cups [650 ml] filtered water

½ tsp sea salt (optional)

Place the rice in a medium bowl and rinse under cool running water, using your hands to gently swish the grains for about 10 seconds. Drain completely.

Pour the filtered water into a heavy-bottomed pot with a tight-fitting lid. Add the rice and salt (if using) and let soak overnight.

Place the pot, uncovered, over medium heat and bring to a boil. The water should bubble around the rim evenly. Cover the pot, turn the heat to very low, and cook, without peeking, for 35 minutes. Remove from the heat and, without opening the lid, let stand for 15 minutes.

Uncover the pot and gently fluff the rice with a rice paddle or wooden spoon. Re-cover and let stand for 5 minutes more. When cool enough to handle, the rice is ready to make onigiri; use immediately.

MAKES ABOUT 5 CUPS [700 G]

ADDING WHOLE GRAINS AND BEANS TO RICE

Mixing whole grains and beans into rice is an ancient Japanese tradition. Millet, barley, Job's tears, and beans have been blended with rice for centuries as a nutritional supplement and to stretch rice in frugal times. Adding whole grains and beans, such as adzuki beans to make red rice, can even be done to celebrate festive occasions. These days, the practice of blending rice with other grains and beans is experiencing a revival. I used to get so excited when my mother threw some pressed barley into the rice, because the rice tasted better and looked prettier.

THE GRAINS AND BEANS PANTRY

It's fun to have a small collection of grains and beans in your cupboard. Make a variety of mixes and add them to your pot of rice. Each grain and bean has its own distinct shape, flavor, quirks, and history. There are infinite varieties to choose from. Visit the farmers' market to buy grains and beans locally from small producers. You will be supporting sustainable agriculture, because these crops are used in their crop rotation to maintain the health of the soils and they also bring cash to the table. Most grains and beans have a shelf life of about a year. Store them in an airtight container in a cool place.

My Favorite Whole-Grain and Bean Mix

I keep glass jars of whole grains and beans in my cupboard, and I must confess I have even more in the pantry. Here are some of my favorites.

Adzuki beans: They are chock-full of B vitamins, minerals, and protein. The addition of adzuki beans will give your rice a pretty pink or burgundy color, depending on the amount you use. Adzuki beans have a distinct nutty flavor and slight bitterness.

Amaranth: The food of the Aztecs, amaranth is high in protein and minerals and has a hint of grassy and peppery flavors.

Buckwheat: There are a lot of benefits to eating and growing buckwheat. It is a fast-growing plant that matures in 75 days and mellows the soil. In Japan, buckwheat is the symbol of a long and lean life. It provides high-quality protein with high levels of rutin, an antioxidant that improves blood circulation. Buckwheat adds a subtle nutty flavor and texture to rice.

Millet: Millet has the smallest seed of the common grains and has a slightly nutty flavor. It is a staple grain in Asia because it is pleasing in flavor, high in protein, and easy to digest.

Quinoa: An ancient grain that was historically cultivated in South America, quinoa has a faintly grassy flavor with a piquant aftertaste. It comes in a variety of earthy colors and is high in protein.

MULTIGRAIN RICE

Use white or haiga rice as the base so the multigrain rice remains sticky enough to make onigiri. This recipe follows the White Rice or Haiga Rice recipe (see page 18), substituting 2 Tbsp of mixed grains and beans for 2 Tbsp of rice. If you want to use brown rice as the base, follow the water-to-rice ratio in the Brown Rice recipe (see page 20). If using an electric rice cooker, pressure cooker, or donabe, follow the manufacturer's instructions.

1¼ cups plus 2 Tbsp [280 g] medium- or short-grain white or haiga rice

2 Tbsp mixed whole grains and beans

½ tsp sea salt (optional)

1¾ cups [420 ml] filtered water

Place the rice in a medium bowl and rinse under cool running water, using your hands to gently swish the grains for about 10 seconds. Drain completely and transfer to a large bowl.

Next, rinse the grains and beans in a strainer and drain. Add the grains and beans and salt (if using) to the rice.

Pour the filtered water into a heavy-bottomed pot with a tight-fitting lid. Add the rice mixture and let soak for 60 minutes, or overnight.

Place the pot, uncovered, over medium heat and bring to a boil. The water should bubble around the rim evenly. Cover the pot, turn the heat to very low, and cook, without peeking, for 20 minutes. Remove from the heat and, without opening the lid, let stand for 15 minutes.

Uncover the pot and gently fluff the rice with a rice paddle or wooden spoon. Re-cover and let stand for 5 minutes more. When cool enough to handle, the rice is ready to make onigiri; use immediately.

MAKES ABOUT 5 CUPS [600 G]

FILLINGS

Onigiri are so versatile that you can make them with almost anything you want. Start with something as simple and practical as the leftover chicken or salmon from last night's dinner. Or pick vegetables and herbs from your garden, rub them with a little salt, and squirt them with lemon juice to make quick pickles for your onigiri. Store-bought capers, olives, and cans of tuna or smoked trout also work well.

No matter which fillings you choose, they should be no more than 20 percent of the onigiri. If your onigiri is made with ¾ cup [90 g] of cooked rice, then use just 1 to 2 Tbsp of filling. You can tuck the filling into the middle of the onigiri, mix it into the rice like a paella, or place it on top like sushi. Avoid oily and watery fillings so your onigiri doesn't get mushy. And use a paper towel, if necessary, to blot any liquid. If your onigiri is large, hold it together with a strip of nori or even a whole lettuce leaf. Pray that it will stay together! And if your large onigiri falls apart, laugh it off and eat it anyway.

SEASONINGS

Onigiri's essential seasoning is salt. I use fine natural sea salt (Shinkai, gray, Celtic). You can find a variety of Japanese sea salts at Japanese markets and online. Besides salt, you can season onigiri with pepper, soy sauce, spices, mayonnaise, citrus zest, broths, and vinegar, to name a few options. There are no rigid rules, except to use seasonings in moderation, so you can taste the natural flavor of the rice. Salt can be cooked with the rice or added afterward. The choice is yours.

FLAVOR AND TEXTURE

You can stimulate your taste buds with so many things: sweet and savory (amakara) braised meat and vegetables sweetened with soy, sweet sake (mirin), and a little sugar; sour (umeboshi); salty (salami, olives); bitter (nuts, brassicas); umami, meaning "pleasant savory taste" (bacon, bonito flakes, smoked mackerel, cheese, pesto); spicy (wasabi, kimchi, cayenne pepper, Sriracha); refreshing and clean (basil, dill, parsley, lemon zest, lemon verbena, shiso, ginger). You can go crunchy (kale chips, burdock, pumpkin seeds, carrots, sunflower seeds) or flowery (nasturtiums, pickled chrysanthemums, pickled cherry blossoms). And as for aroma, you can select from quite a range (toasted sesame, paprika, black pepper, Madras curry powder, saffron, cumin). I will show you how to make fillings that can be prepared ahead of time or just before you assemble your onigiri.

FURIKAKE

Traditional furikake is the savory "confetti" that's sprinkled on top of the onigiri or mixed into the rice for added flavor and crunch. It can be completely dry or a little moist. It can also be sprinkled onto grilled vegetables, seafood, eggs, and meats. Furikake can be a single element, like toasted sesame seeds, or a combination of ingredients as varied as sea salt, nori, bonito flakes, dried anchovies, dried cod roe, dried egg, dried shrimp, dried herbs, dried vegetables and citrus rinds, nuts, Japanese red chile peppers, and sansho pepper, as well as poppy, sesame, and other seeds. Though you can buy containers of colorful furikake at Japanese markets and online, it's fun and easy to make furikake at home. If you are buying furikake, look for blends that don't contain any food coloring or chemical preservatives.

TOASTING SESAME SEEDS

To toast sesame seeds, put them in a wide frying pan over medium heat. Toast the seeds, stirring with a spatula, until they turn fragrant and a few seeds start to pop, about 2 minutes. Be careful not to burn the seeds. Remove from the heat and pour onto a metal baking sheet to let cool.

KALE FURIKAKE

My friend Mamiko Nishiyama is the proprietor of Yagicho, a 280-year-old shop in Tokyo that specializes in dried bonito and dehydrated seaweed and vegetables, the ingredients for making the Japanese stock called dashi. We collaborated on a dashi-themed pop-up dinner with chefs Nick Balla and Cortney Burns at Bar Tartine in San Francisco. Mamiko and I were in charge of making onigiri. Cortney gave us dehydrated kale leaves and wild nori harvested from the coast of Mendocino to use in the furikake. We were familiar with wild nori, but neither of us had ever used kale to make furikake. We concocted a furikake made with bonito flakes, kale, wild nori, and sesame seeds and mixed it into the rice and sprinkled some on top. It was a hit! This recipe is a vegetarian furikake, so there are no bonito flakes. If you want to get adventurous like we did at Bar Tartine, combine bonito flakes with Kale Furikake.

8 kale leaves, stemmed

1 strip lemon or any citrus peel, about ½ by 2 in [12 mm by 5 cm], pith removed

½ sheet nori

½ Japanese dried red chile, seeded and minced (optional)

2 Tbsp black sesame seeds, toasted (see page 27)

2 Tbsp white sesame seeds, toasted (see page 27)

¼ tsp freshly ground black pepper or sansho pepper

½ tsp sea salt, or to taste

Preheat the oven to 175°F [80°C], then lower the oven temperature to 150°F [65°C].

Put the kale leaves and lemon peel on a baking

sheet. Bake until the kale and lemon peel are completely dehydrated and brittle, 6 to 8 hours.

Pass the kale leaves through a fine-mesh sieve, breaking them up with your hands and then pressing them through with a spatula or spoon to achieve an irregular, not-too-fine texture. Set the lemon peel aside.

In a skillet over low heat, cook the nori until crisp, flipping once, about 1 minute. Remove from the heat and let cool. Crumble the nori into small pieces and set aside.

Transfer the lemon peel and chile (if using) to a food processor or spice grinder and pulse a few times, until they turn into fine (not powdery) flakes. Be careful not to overprocess; some of the flakiness should remain intact. Add the kale, nori, sesame seeds, black pepper, and salt to the food processor or grinder and pulse four or five times, until they turn into a coarse powder.

Store in an airtight container in a cool, dark place for up to 1 month.

MAKES ¾ CUP [45 G]

SESAME FURIKAKE

There is a reason that sesame furikake is the king of all furikakes. It's versatile, has great texture and nutty flavor, and is an excellent source of minerals and fiber. To make your own, use a Japanese mortar and pestle (called a *suribachi* and *surikogi*). The ridged interior of a Japanese mortar works efficiently to grind sesame seeds. If you don't have time to grind the sesame seeds, just use them whole. Most sesame seeds sold in Asian markets are toasted, but they taste better if you toast them again.

½ cup [70 g] white or black sesame seeds, toasted (see page 27)

1 tsp sea salt

Put the sesame seeds in a Japanese mortar and grind with a Japanese pestle until the seeds are coarsely ground. You can also use a spice or coffee grinder and pulse a few times until coarsely ground (you should see a few whole seeds in the mixture). Stir in the salt.

Store in an airtight container in a cool, dark place for up to 1 month.

MAKES ½ CUP [75 G]

SHAPiNG

Onigiri have five basic shapes: ball, triangular, log, disc, and envelope. My mother and grandmother made onigiri in triangles. And so I do, too, though I flirted briefly with round shapes because they are so easy to form. I remember a boy who would come to school with cannonball-shaped onigiri. His father, a single dad, made them. That boy always brought three dried sardines to go with his big, round onigiri.

I like to keep the ball and log onigiri small, using ⅓ cup [50 g] of rice, so they can be eaten in just a couple of bites.

SHAPING BY HAND

Now it's your turn to make onigiri. You can make it into any shape or size you like, but read through the fundamentals first and have a fresh pot of cooked rice at the ready. When shaping your onigiri, always start with clean hands and fresh rice. Do not use any perfumed soap to wash your hands, as the smell will transfer into the rice. If the rice is too hot, let it cool off a little before you handle it.

Pour 1 cup [240 ml] of water into a small bowl to moisten your hands, and put 2 tsp fine sea salt in another small bowl. These will be used for dipping your hands and keeping the rice from sticking to them.

Scoop about ¾ cup [100 g] of cooked rice into a small teacup or bowl. If including a filling, use your fingers (it doesn't matter which fingers are used here) to press an indentation into the rice. Place the filling into the indentation and mold the rice around it.

Moisten your hands with the water to keep the rice from sticking to them. Lightly dip the tips of the index, middle, and ring fingers of one hand into the bowl of water, then into the bowl of sea salt. Rub the salt onto your palms. You should have a light coating on your palms; as you continue to make onigiri you will develop a sense for how much salt you like to add.

Gently tap the teacup or bowl to loosen the rice into your palm. Cup one hand to hold the rice and continue with the following instructions for making specific shapes.

Ball: An onigiri ball is so easy to make that you probably don't need me to tell you how. Just make sure the rice covers the filling, and gently shape it into a ball.

Triangular: Mold the rice to form a ball and cup one hand to hold it. Press gently with your other hand, cupping your hand around the rice, to create one corner of the triangular shape. Using your index finger, middle finger, and thumb as a guide, press the sides. Turn the ball and repeat a couple more times to give the onigiri three corners and three flat sides; it will be about 1 in [2.5 cm] thick. The onigiri should be firm on the outside and fluffy on the inside.

Log: Mold the rice to make a ball and hold it in one hand. Press it gently into your palm, using the index finger, middle finger, and thumb of your other hand to gently press the two ends of the ball to form a "log." Now use your index finger, middle finger, and thumb to complete the log shape, without squashing the log.

Disc: Mold the rice to make a ball, then use your fingers to gently flatten into a disc; it will be about 1 in (2.5 cm) thick.

Envelope: This onigiri is folded like a burrito. The rice and the fillings are wrapped in nori instead of a flour tortilla. It's called *onigirazu* in Japanese, which means "no molding." Place a sheet of nori at a diagonal on a work surface, shiny-side down. Spread ¼ cup [40 g] of cooked rice in the center of the nori. Sprinkle with a pinch of salt. Add your fillings, perhaps a thin layer of mayo, a slice of ham or cheese or a scrambled egg, and a small piece of lettuce, and cover with another ¼ cup [40 g] of rice. Sprinkle with another pinch of salt. (Put in enough filling to fill about one-fourth of the nori sheet at most.) Carefully fold the sides of the nori toward the center so they touch, and press down with your fingers. With the sides folded in, bring the top and bottom corners to the center, similar to the way you wrap a present, so that the rice and the fillings don't spill out. Flip the onigiri, seam-side down. Finally, moisten a sharp knife with a well-wrung wet towel and slice the onigiri in half. It should look like a sandwich that's made with nori instead of bread.

Freestyle: You can make onigiri in almost any shape you can think of. Children adore freestyle onigiri and they are also great at parties.

USING ONIGIRI MOLDS

Wooden and plastic onigiri molds come in all sizes and shapes: triangle, oval, star, panda, flower, even a car. I own triangular and oval molds, which I find quite useful when I'm making a lot of onigiri and don't have enough helping hands. (You can find onigiri molds in Japanese markets and online.) To prevent the rice from sticking to the mold, always wet it lightly before use.

Even when using a mold, be sure to finish shaping onigiri by hand. This will breathe some soul into it—and is the secret of good onigiri. Another secret is to cover the rice with plastic wrap. It's less messy and you won't have to worry about the rice being too hot. Just cut out a large enough piece of plastic wrap to drape over a teacup. Put the rice and the filling into the plastic-lined teacup. Gather the plastic and lift the onigiri out of the teacup with your hands. Twist the ends of the plastic wrap and mold the rice into any shape you like. Unwrap the plastic and give the onigiri a final press with your slightly wet, salted hands.

WRAPPING ONIGIRI

The most common wrapper for onigiri is nori. It not only holds the onigiri together, but also adds flavor and nutrition. Pickled greens, leaves, crêpes, or slices of meat can be used to wrap onigiri.

NORI

This soft, crispy dried black seaweed comes in large sheets or bite-size rectangular pieces. All nori are not the same. They are sold in grades, which range from rejects to premium nori from the Ariake Sea, off the island of Kyushu, Japan. Good nori is crisp, thick, aromatic, and dissolves nicely in your mouth. You can also purchase seasoned nori, but make sure you approve of the additives. Some nori is seasoned with fragrant sesame oil, sugar, and spices.

LEAFY VEGETABLES AND OTHER WRAPPERS

Leafy vegetables, pickled leafy greens, rice paper, and other seaweeds, like Oboro konbu, also make nice wrappers. I am particularly fond of fresh Swiss chard. If you prefer softer leaves, give them a quick blanch, but be sure to pat them dry.

TIPS ON CUTTING, TOASTING, AND STORING NORI

You can cut nori into halves, thirds (lengthwise or crosswise), eighths, or sixteenths. Cut them on a diagonal, or use a whole sheet to wrap your onigiri. I once saw a child make butterfly wings with nori. Always place the shiny side facedown when making your onigiri, so the prettier side shows.

Once the onigiri is wrapped, the nori will pick up moisture from the rice and go limp. Onigiri is best when the nori is crispy, so I like to keep the nori separate from the onigiri and wrap it just before I eat it.

Most nori comes toasted, but you can make it crispier by waving each sheet over a medium-hot flame for a few seconds or in a hot skillet until green and crispy. Nori must be stored in airtight containers to avoid exposure to moisture. Nori can keep in a dry place for several months but will taste best when fresh, so use it up right away.

YOUR FIRST
ONIGIRI

This onigiri will teach you how to build flavors. The fillings are peas and umeboshi, also known as salt plums. You can omit the umeboshi and just serve the onigiri plain. If you wrap your onigiri but want your nori to stay crisp, keep it separate from the onigiri and wrap it just before you eat.

2 sheets or 6 bite-size rectangular pieces nori

1 cup [240 ml] water

2½ tsp sea salt

¾ cup [100 g] fresh or frozen peas or edamame

6 umeboshi, pitted and chopped (optional)

2 Tbsp minced peeled ginger

1 recipe White Rice or Haiga Rice (page 18), Brown Rice (page 20), or Multigrain Rice (page 24)

3 Tbsp Sesame Furikake (page 30)

If wrapping the onigiri, cut each nori sheet lengthwise into three strips. Set aside in a dry place.

In a small saucepan over high heat, bring the water and ½ tsp of the salt to a boil. Add the peas and cook for 1 minute. Drain and set aside in a small bowl.

cont'd

Have ready a large plate or cutting board to hold the finished onigiri. Prepare a small bowl of water for wetting your hands, a small bowl containing the remaining 2 tsp salt, and a bowl containing the umeboshi (if using). Arrange near the plate.

Fold the peas and ginger into the rice, combining gently, without mashing the grains.

Divide the rice into six equal portions. Scoop one portion into a small teacup or bowl.

Using your fingers (it doesn't matter which fingers are used here), press an indentation into the rice. Add one-sixth of the chopped umeboshi into the indentation and mold the rice around it.

Moisten your hands with the water to keep the rice from sticking to them. Lightly dip the tips of the index, middle, and ring fingers of one hand into the bowl of water, then into the bowl of salt. Rub the salt onto your palms. You should have a light coating on your palms.

Gently tap the teacup or bowl to loosen the rice into your palm. Cup one hand to hold the rice ball. Press gently with your other hand, cupping your hand around the rice, to create one corner of the triangular shape. Using your index finger, middle finger, and thumb as a guide, press the sides. Turn the ball and repeat a couple more times to give the onigiri three corners and three flat sides; it will be about 1 in [2.5 cm] thick. Don't press too hard; the onigiri should be firm on the outside but soft and airy on the inside. Place the finished onigiri on the prepared plate. Repeat with the remaining ingredients.

Hold an onigiri in one hand and wrap a piece of nori around it like a robe, starting at the back of the triangle and ending in front. Press gently to fix the nori in place. Repeat with the remaining onigiri and nori. (If you are using the rectangular pieces, wrap a piece of nori around the center at the triangle.) Sprinkle with the furikake.

Eat immediately, wrap tightly in plastic and store at room temperature for up to 6 hours, or refrigerate for up to 12 hours. If refrigerating, microwave to warm before serving.

MAKES 6 TRIANGULAR ONIGIRI

GRILLED ONIGIRI
WITH SOY SAUCE

Onigiri taste heavenly when toasted on the grill, and *yaki onigiri* (grilled onigiri) are popular in *izakayas*, the convivial bars for eating and drinking that are popular in Japan. Exposed to heat, a rich filling such as butter, cheese, or bacon will melt and flavor the surrounding rice. If you want to give your onigiri a little kick, baste with chili oil instead of light sesame oil. If you want to add more umami, baste with miso or barbecue sauce. Most of the recipes in this book can turn into yaki onigiri if you omit the nori and put them on the grill.

1 recipe White Rice or Haiga Rice (page 18), Brown Rice (page 20), or Multigrain Rice (page 24)

¼ cup [60 ml] soy sauce

¼ cup [60 ml] sesame oil or chili oil

Have ready a large plate or cutting board to hold the finished onigiri. Prepare a small bowl of water for wetting your hands. Arrange near the plate.

Divide the rice into six equal portions. Scoop one portion into a small teacup or bowl.

Moisten your hands with the water to keep the rice from sticking to them.

Gently tap the teacup or bowl to loosen the rice into your palm. Cup one hand to hold the rice ball. Press gently with your other hand, cupping your hand around the rice, to create one corner of the triangular shape. Using your index finger, middle finger, and thumb as a guide, press the sides. Turn the ball and repeat a couple more times to give the onigiri

43

cont'd

three corners and three flat sides; it will be about 1 in [2.5 cm] thick. Don't press too hard; the onigiri should be firm on the outside but soft and airy on the inside. Place the finished onigiri on the prepared plate. Repeat with the remaining ingredients.

Prepare a charcoal grill, set a gas grill to medium, place a grill pan over medium-high heat, or position an oven rack 6 in [15 cm] from the heat source and preheat the broiler. Line a baking sheet (if using) with aluminum foil.

Place the soy sauce in a small bowl next to the grill.

Brush the onigiri lightly on both sides with the sesame oil to prevent them from sticking to the grill.

Grill the onigiri until crisp and toasted, 5 to 10 minutes per side, depending on the heat. While grilling, baste with soy sauce a few times; the sauce should be absorbed and the onigiri should not be moist.

Eat immediately with a fork if you like, or wait till it cools off slightly and eat with your fingers.

MAKES 6 TRIANGULAR ONIGIRI

STORING AND REHEATING ONIGIRI

Onigiri taste best when they are made with freshly cooked rice and eaten immediately after forming or grilling. They can also be enjoyed at room temperature later in the day. When onigiri are refrigerated, the rice hardens and loses flavor. I usually use hardened onigiri to make fried rice, but you can also reheat them by steaming for a couple of minutes, or covering with a moistened paper towel and microwaving on high until warm, about 30 seconds. If your onigiri fall apart, reshape them or eat with a fork. If your onigiri is wrapped with nori or greens, these will get mushy when reheated; wrap the onigiri after it has been reheated.

CHAPTER TWO:
RECIPES

In this chapter, we will make vegetarian, seafood, and meat-filled or -topped onigiri. I have also sprinkled in some recipes for breakfast onigiri, whimsical onigiri, and some traditional sides.

Use these recipes to learn technique and spur your own creativity; once you master onigiri, you can start mixing and matching fillings, toppings, wraps, and rice mixtures. For example, you can make Amakara Chicken Onigiri (page 85) and put it on the grill, using the method for Grilled Onigiri with Soy Sauce (page 43).

In some of these recipes, the fillings are folded into the rice like a pilaf. Some are onigiri with fillings in their centers, and some are topped like sushi.

You can pickle, steam, sauté, or grill vegetables and use them as onigiri fillings. When I see the first fava beans at the farmers' market in spring, I get excited about making onigiri with them. I love to add fresh herbs and other aromatics such as shiso, basil, dill, parsley, cilantro, ginger, lemon peel, and sesame to my onigiri to brighten flavors.

Pairing rice with seafood is traditional in Japanese cuisine, and many people put nigiri sushi in the same category as onigiri, because it is molded by hand. Though nigiri sushi takes many years of hard work and discipline to master, you don't have to undergo such training to become good at making seafood onigiri. I love seafood, but I am mindful about what I eat these days. I follow the Monterey Bay Aquarium Seafood Watch to see which fish are caught or farmed in ways that cause little harm to habitats and wildlife.

DRIED FRUIT AND NUT
"TOAST" ONIGIRI

I shared this onigiri with a Japanese friend, who thought it was weird. But it's delicious as is or spread with butter and jam. Some possible riffs include almond butter and honey or peanut butter and grape jelly. You can use other nuts or seeds (almonds, walnuts, peanuts, sunflower seeds) and dried fruits (cranberries, raisins, blueberries, figs). It's perfect for breakfast; as an afternoon snack, it goes well with cold milk, coffee, tea, or miso soup.

2 tsp sea salt

¼ cup [40 g] chopped dried apricots

¼ cup [40 g] chopped raisins

¼ cup [25 g] chopped pecans

1 recipe White Rice or Haiga Rice (page 18), Brown Rice (page 20), or Multigrain Rice (page 24)

¼ cup [115 g] blueberry jam (optional)

2 Tbsp melted butter

Have ready a large plate or cutting board to hold the finished onigiri. Prepare a small bowl of water for wetting your hands and a small bowl containing the salt. Arrange near the plate.

Fold the apricots, raisins, and pecans into the rice, combining gently, without mashing the grains.

Divide the rice into six equal portions. Scoop one portion into a small teacup or bowl. Using your fingers (it doesn't matter which fingers are used here), press an indentation into the rice. Add 1 tsp of the jam into the indentation and mold the rice around it.

Moisten your hands with the water to keep the rice from sticking to them. Lightly dip the tips of the index, middle, and ring fingers of one hand into the bowl of water, then into the bowl of salt. Rub the salt onto your palms. You should have a light coating on your palms.

Gently tap the teacup or bowl to loosen the rice into your palm. Cup one hand to hold the rice ball. Press gently with your other hand, cupping your hand around the rice, to create one corner of the triangular shape. Using your index finger, middle finger, and thumb as a guide, press the sides. Turn the ball and repeat a couple more times to give the onigiri three corners and three flat sides; it will be about 1 in [2.5 cm] thick. Don't press too hard; the onigiri should be firm on the outside but soft and airy on the inside. Place the finished onigiri on the prepared plate. Repeat with the remaining ingredients.

Position an oven rack about 6 in [15 cm] from the heat source and preheat the broiler. Line a baking sheet with aluminum foil.

Brush the onigiri on both sides with the butter and place them on the prepared baking sheet.

Broil the onigiri until crisp and toasted, about 3 minutes per side.

Eat immediately with a fork if you like, or wait till it cools off slightly and eat with your fingers.

MAKES 6 TRIANGULAR ONIGIRI

PiCKLED RADISH ONIGIRI

Ume plum vinegar is available at gourmet supermarkets, health food stores, and online. If you cannot find ume plum vinegar, use rice vinegar. The pickled radishes taste great by themselves and would make a nice side dish, or use the slices to garnish your onigiri, as I've done here. I use beet to dye the radish pink. You can omit that step.

8 red or white radishes, cut crosswise into ⅟₁₆-in [2-mm] slices

½ cup [120 ml] sushi vinegar (page 119)

1 beet, cut crosswise into ⅟₁₆-in [2-mm] slices (optional)

2 tsp sea salt

3 Tbsp chopped parsley

1 tsp lemon zest

1 recipe White Rice or Haiga Rice (page 18), Brown Rice (page 20), or Multigrain Rice (page 24)

3 Tbsp Sesame Furikake (page 30)

In a bowl, combine the radishes with the sushi vinegar and beet (if using) and refrigerate for 1 to 3 hours.

Remove the pickled radishes from the vinegar and drain well. Set aside twelve slices to decorate the top of your onigiri, if you like. Cut the slices into ⅟₁₆-in [2-mm] dice. Blot dry with paper towels. Eat the beet slices as a snack.

Have ready a large plate or cutting board to hold the finished onigiri. Prepare

cont'd

a small bowl of water for wetting your hands and a small bowl containing the salt. Arrange near the plate.

Fold the diced radish, parsley, and lemon zest into the rice, combining gently, without mashing the grains.

Divide the rice into twelve equal portions. Scoop one portion into a small teacup or bowl.

Moisten your hands with the water to keep the rice from sticking to them. Lightly dip the tips of the index, middle, and ring fingers of one hand into the bowl of water, then into the bowl of salt. Rub the salt onto your palms. You

should have a light coating on your palms.

Gently tap the teacup or bowl to loosen the rice into your palm. Press gently into your palm, then use the index finger, middle finger, and thumb of your other hand to gently press the two ends of the ball to form a log, about 1½ in [4 cm] wide and 2½ in [6 cm] long. Now use your index finger, middle finger, and thumb to complete the log shape. Don't press too hard; the onigiri should be firm on the outside but soft and airy in the inside. Place the finished onigiri on the prepared plate. Repeat with the remaining ingredients.

Cut a slit halfway through a slice of radish, without cutting it in half. Twist the slice to make a butterfly shape. Repeat with remaining slices.

Sprinkle the onigiri with the furikake and top each with a radish twist.

Eat immediately.

MAKES 12 LOG ONIGIRI

HIJIKI, CARROT, AND SHIITAKE ONIGIRI

This combination is a crunchy delight of sweet carrot, meaty shiitake, and mildly briny hijiki seaweed. The Japanese believe that eating seaweed results in shiny hair and good skin.

1½ Tbsp sesame oil

1 carrot, peeled and shredded

2 dried shiitake mushrooms, soaked in 1 cup [240 ml] water overnight and drained

⅓ cup [10 g] hijiki seaweed, rinsed, soaked in 2 cups [480 ml] water for at least 3 hours or up to overnight, and drained

1 Tbsp soy sauce

1 Tbsp sake

1 Tbsp mirin

½ tsp cane sugar

2 tsp minced ginger

2 tsp sea salt

1 recipe White Rice or Haiga Rice (page 18), Brown Rice (page 20), or Multigrain Rice (page 24)

2 Tbsp Kale Furikake (page 28) or Sesame Furikake (page 30)

In a large, nonstick frying pan over medium heat, warm the sesame oil. Add the carrot, mushrooms, and hijiki and cook, stirring often, until the vegetables are limp, about 4 minutes. Add the soy sauce, sake, mirin, sugar, and ginger; turn the heat to low; and cook until most of the liquid is absorbed, 4 to 5 minutes more. Remove from the heat and let cool. Chop coarsely, so that the hijiki and mushroom pieces are about ¼ in [6 mm] in

cont'd

length. (The filling keeps for up to 5 days in the refrigerator. Let come to room temperature before adding to the rice.)

Have ready a large plate or cutting board to hold the finished onigiri. Prepare a small bowl of water for wetting your hands and a small bowl containing the salt. Arrange near the plate.

Cut out a large piece of plastic wrap and drape over a small teacup or bowl.

Fold 6 Tbsp [20 g] of the vegetable mixture into the rice, combining gently, without mashing the grains. (You will have some leftover vegetables; enjoy as a side dish.)

Divide the rice into six equal portions. Scoop one portion into the plastic-lined teacup or bowl.

Moisten your hands with the water to keep the rice from sticking to them. Lightly dip the tips of the index, middle, and ring fingers of one hand into the bowl of water, then into the bowl of salt. Rub the salt onto your palms. You should have a light coating on your palms.

Gather the plastic wrap and lift the onigiri out of the teacup with your hands. Twist the ends of the plastic wrap and mold the rice into a ball. Unwrap the plastic, remove the onigiri, and give it a

gentle final press with your slightly wet hands. Don't press too hard; the onigiri should be firm on the outside but soft and airy on the inside. Place the finished onigiri on the prepared plate. Repeat with the remaining ingredients. Sprinkle with the furikake.

Eat immediately, wrap tightly in plastic and store at room temperature for up to 6 hours, or refrigerate for up to 12 hours. If refrigerating, microwave to warm before serving.

MAKES 6 BALL ONIGIRI

AVOCADO, SOY, WASABI, CHARD
WRAP ONIGIRI

This onigiri is folded like an envelope (see page 33). The rice and fillings are wrapped in chard instead of nori. Add crabmeat and this becomes a California onigiri. Top with chopped fresh cilantro or chives, if you want a little bite. I have grown to love the flavor and texture of fresh leafy greens and was inspired to create this recipe. With the dipping sauce, these chard wraps make a good vegan appetizer.

10 Swiss chard leaves

2 Tbsp soy sauce

2 tsp freshly grated wasabi or wasabi paste

2½ ripe avocados, pitted, peeled, and sliced into 30 wedges

2 tsp sea salt

4 Tbsp chopped fresh cilantro

1 tsp freshly grated lime zest

1 recipe White Rice or Haiga Rice (page 18), Brown Rice (page 20), or Multigrain Rice (page 24)

SOY VINEGAR DIPPING SAUCE
4 Tbsp sesame oil

4 Tbsp soy sauce

4 Tbsp Sushi Vinegar (page 119)

1 tsp Sesame Furikake (page 30) or Kale Furikake (page 28)

1 tsp freshly grated lime zest

Using a chef's knife, cut out the thick ribs of the chard leaves. Dry the leaves with paper towels and set aside.

In a small bowl, stir together the soy sauce and wasabi. Fold in the avocado, without mashing it.

Have ready a large plate or cutting board to hold the finished onigiri. Prepare a small bowl of water for wetting your hands, a small bowl containing the salt, and the bowl of avocado. Arrange near the plate.

Fold the cilantro and lime zest into the rice, combining gently, without mashing the grains.

Place a chard leaf on a work surface, leafy green part up. Spread ¼ cup [40 g] of rice in the center of the leaf. Cover with one-tenth of the avocado, followed by another ¼ cup [40 g] of rice. Carefully, fold the sides of the chard toward the center, then bring the top and bottom to the center. Flip seam-side down. Cut in half crosswise. Repeat with the remaining ingredients.

To make the dipping sauce:
In a small bowl, stir together the sesame oil, soy sauce, vinegar, furikake, and lime zest.

Eat immediately with the dipping sauce, or wrap tightly in plastic and store at room temperature for up to 6 hours, or refrigerate for up to 12 hours.

MAKES 10 ENVELOPE ONIGIRI

SWEET POTATO AND BLACK SESAME ONIGIRI

This is a classic onigiri, made slightly modern with the use of butter. If you can't find *satsumaimo* (yellow sweet potato), use another variety of sweet potato.

1½ cups [300 g] uncooked medium- or short-grain white rice, haiga rice, or mixed-grain rice

1¾ cups [420 ml] filtered water

2 Tbsp butter

8 oz [230 g] satsumaimo or other sweet potato, unpeeled, cut into ¼-in [6-mm] cubes

One 4-in [10-cm] piece konbu seaweed

2 Tbsp sake

1 Tbsp mirin

2½ tsp sea salt

3 Tbsp black sesame seeds, toasted (see page 27)

1 sheet nori

Place the rice in a medium bowl and rinse under cool running water, using your hands to gently swish the grains for about 10 seconds. Drain completely.

Pour the filtered water into a heavy-bottomed pot with a tight-fitting lid. Add the

rice and let soak for about 30 minutes.

In a frying pan over medium heat, melt the butter. Add the sweet potato and sauté until slightly brown, about 3 minutes.

Add the konbu, sake, mirin, sweet potato, and ½ tsp of the salt to the rice and stir until combined.

Place the pot, uncovered, over medium heat and bring to a boil. The water should bubble around the rim evenly. Cover the pot,

cont'd

turn the heat to very low, and cook, without peeking, for 20 minutes. Remove from the heat and, without opening the lid, let stand for 15 minutes.

Uncover the pot and gently fluff the rice with a rice paddle or wooden spoon. Re-cover and let stand for 5 minutes more. Remove the konbu (enjoy it as a snack). Fold the toasted sesame seeds into the rice, combining gently, without mashing the grains. When cool enough to handle, the rice is ready to make onigiri.

Cut the nori crosswise into twelve strips, each ¾ by 4 in [2 by 10 cm]; these are for wrapping the onigiri. Set aside in a dry place.

Have ready a large plate or cutting board to hold the finished onigiri. Prepare a small bowl of water for wetting your hands and a small bowl containing the remaining 2 tsp salt. Arrange near the plate.

Divide the rice into twelve equal portions. Scoop one portion into a small teacup or bowl.

Moisten your hands with the water to keep the rice from sticking to them. Lightly dip the tips of the index, middle, and ring fingers of one hand into the bowl of water, then into the bowl of salt. Rub the salt onto your palms. You should have a light coating on your palms.

Gently tap the teacup or bowl to loosen the rice into your palm. Press gently into your palm, then use the index finger, middle finger, and thumb of your other hand to gently press the two ends of the ball to form a log, about 1½ in [4 cm] wide and 2½ in [6 cm] long. Now use your index finger, middle finger, and thumb to complete the log shape. Don't press too hard; the onigiri should be firm on the outside but soft and airy on the inside.

Place the finished onigiri on the prepared plate. Repeat with the remaining ingredients.

Hold an onigiri in one hand and wrap a piece of nori around it like a belt, starting at the center and wrapping around the log. Press gently to fix the nori in place. Repeat with the remaining onigiri and nori.

Eat immediately.

MAKES 12 LOG ONIGIRI

CURRiED
FRIED RICE ONiGiRI

In the olden days, onigiri were often dyed with yellow food coloring using *kuchi-nashi*, a Japanese gardenia seed pod, to make them stand out at roadside stands. My mother used to make a quick fried rice with Green Giant's frozen carrots, green beans, and peas, and sometimes, she would throw in some curry powder to make yellow onigiri. My recipe is a variation of hers, and it's just as colorful. Throw in some shrimp or chicken, too, if you like.

1 sheet nori

2 Tbsp vegetable oil

1 carrot, peeled and diced

½ yellow onion, minced

1 green bell pepper, diced

1 tsp Madras curry powder

2 Tbsp butter

1 recipe White Rice or Haiga Rice (page 18), Brown Rice (page 20), or Multigrain Rice (page 24)

Sea salt (optional)

Freshly ground black pepper

2 Tbsp Sesame Furikake (page 30)

Cut the nori lengthwise into ten strips; these are for wrapping the onigiri. Set aside in a dry place.

Have ready a large plate or cutting board to hold the finished onigiri. Prepare a small bowl of water for wetting your hands. Arrange near the plate.

In a large, nonstick frying pan or well-seasoned wok over medium heat, warm the vegetable oil. Add the carrot and onion and cook, stirring often, until the vegetables are limp, about 4 minutes. Add the bell pepper and stir-fry for 1 minute more. Turn the heat to low, add the curry powder, and stir constantly for about 1 minute. Turn the heat to medium and add the butter. When the butter has melted, add the rice, combining gently, without mashing the grains, until you get an even yellow color. Add ½ tsp salt (unless you already added salt when cooking the rice) and ¼ tsp black pepper and adjust the seasoning to your liking. When cool enough to handle, the rice is ready to make onigiri.

Cut out a large piece of plastic wrap and drape over a small teacup or bowl.

Divide the fried rice into ten equal portions. Scoop one portion into the plastic-lined teacup or bowl.

Moisten your hands with the water to keep the rice from sticking to them.

Gather the plastic wrap and lift the onigiri out of the teacup with your hands. Twist the ends of the plastic wrap and mold the rice into a ball. Unwrap the plastic, remove the onigiri, and give it a gentle final press with your slightly wet hands. Don't press too hard; the onigiri should be firm on

the outside but soft and airy on the inside. Place the finished onigiri on the prepared plate. Repeat with the remaining ingredients.

Hold an onigiri in one hand and wrap a piece of nori around it. Press gently to fix the nori in place. Repeat with the remaining onigiri and nori. Sprinkle with the furikake.

Eat immediately.

MAKES 10 BALL ONIGIRI

SPICY
SCALLOP ONIGIRI

Scallops lend their tenderness and good flavor to the rice. These little scallops may slip out of your onigiri, so put them on top or wrap a piece of nori around the rice. The Spicy Furikake adds another layer or spice and texture.

5 oz [140 g] scallops, washed and dried

Sea salt

1 Tbsp butter

1 tsp sesame oil

1 Tbsp soy sauce

1 Tbsp sake

1 Tbsp mirin

1 sheet nori

SPICY FURIKAKE
½ tsp Madras curry powder

¼ tsp freshly ground black pepper

⅛ tsp cayenne pepper

2 Tbsp Sesame Furikake (page 30)

⅓ cup [15 g] chopped fresh chives

1 recipe White Rice or Haiga Rice (page 18), Brown Rice (page 20), or Multigrain Rice (page 24)

Season the scallops with salt, and cut any large pieces into ½-in [12-mm] squares.

In a 12-in [30.5-cm] sauté pan over high heat, warm the butter and sesame oil. When the oil begins to smoke, add the scallops and sear for about 1 minute on each side. Do not move the scallops around while searing, they should be browned on each side and translucent in the center. Add the soy sauce, sake, and mirin and

cont'd

cook for 1 minute more. Remove from heat and let cool to room temperature. (The scallops will keep for 2 days in the refrigerator. Bring to room temperature before using.)

Cut the nori lengthwise into six strips; these are for wrapping the onigiri. Set aside in a dry place.

To make the spicy furikake
In a small bowl, stir together the curry powder, black pepper, cayenne, and furikake. Set aside.

Have ready a large plate or cutting board to hold the finished onigiri. Prepare a small bowl of water for wetting your hands and a small bowl containing 2 tsp salt. Arrange near the plate.

Fold the chives and scallops into the rice, combining gently, without mashing the grains.

Divide the rice into six equal portions. Scoop one portion into a small teacup or bowl.

Moisten your hands with the water to keep the rice from sticking to them. Lightly dip the tips of the index, middle, and ring fingers of one hand into the bowl of water, then into the bowl of salt. Rub the salt onto your palms. You should have a light coating on your palms.

Gently tap the teacup or bowl to loosen the rice into your palm. Mold the rice to make a ball, then use your fingers to gently flatten into a disc about 2¾ in (7 cm) thick. Don't press too hard; the onigiri should be firm on the outside but soft and airy on the inside. The small scallops may slip out of the onigiri; try to push them back inside, without mashing the rice. Place the finished onigiri on the prepared plate. Repeat with the remaining ingredients.

Hold an onigiri in one hand and wrap a piece of nori around the edge of the disc. Press gently to fix the nori in place. Repeat with the remaining onigiri and nori. Sprinkle with the furikake.

Eat immediately.

MAKES 6 DISC ONIGIRI

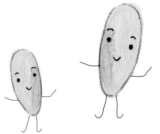

SHRIMP TEMPURA ONIGIRI

Called *tenmusu*, this popular shrimp tempura onigiri originated in Nagoya Prefecture. Wrap the rice around the shrimp, leaving their cute little tails sticking out.

6 medium shrimp or prawns

1¼ cups [150 g] cake flour

2 Tbsp cornstarch, plus more as needed

1 cup [240 ml] ice water

1 egg yolk, beaten

Canola, peanut, or corn oil for frying

2 sheets nori

2 tsp sea salt

1 recipe White Rice or Haiga Rice (page 18), Brown Rice (page 20), or Multigrain Rice (page 24)

Onigiri Egg Dipping Sauce (see page 113)

3 Tbsp Sesame Furikake (page 30; optional)

Rinse and peel the shrimp, leaving the tails intact. Devein the shrimp and make three slits crosswise along the underside of each one to keep them from shrinking and curling up while frying.

Sift the flour with the cornstarch into a small bowl. In a medium bowl, combine the ice water with the egg yolk. Add the sifted flour to the egg mixture and whisk together. Don't whisk too much, as the batter should have some small lumps. Check the consistency of

cont'd

the batter; if it is too thin, add more cornstarch to thicken.

Pour enough canola oil into a 2-qt [2-L] cast-iron pot to come 2 to 3 in [5 to 7.5 cm] up the sides. Heat over medium-high heat until an instant-read thermometer reads 325°F [165°C].

Working in batches, pick up the tail of a shrimp with your hand, dip the shrimp into the batter, and gently drop it into the hot oil. You can fry two or three shrimp at a time.

Fry the shrimp on all sides until the batter is crisp, 1 to 2 minutes. Remove with a slotted spoon and drain on paper towels. Repeat until

all the shrimp are fried, checking the oil temperature before frying each batch. Set the shrimp aside and let cool.

Cut each nori sheet crosswise into three strips; these are for wrapping the onigiri. Set aside in a dry place.

Have ready a large plate or cutting board to hold the finished onigiri. Prepare a small bowl of water for wetting your hands and a small bowl containing the salt. Arrange near the plate.

Divide the rice into six equal portions. Scoop one portion into a small teacup or bowl. Using your fingers (it doesn't matter which fingers are used here),

press an indentation into the rice. Dip a shrimp in the dipping sauce, then place into the indentation, with the tail sticking up, and mold the rice around it.

Moisten your hands with the water to keep the rice from sticking to them. Lightly dip the tips of the index, middle, and ring fingers of one hand into the bowl of water, then into the bowl of salt. Rub the salt onto your palms. You should have a light coating on your palms.

Gently tap the teacup or bowl to loosen the rice into your palm. Cup one hand to hold the rice ball. Press gently with your other hand, cupping your hand around the rice, to create one corner of the triangular shape. (Leave the shrimp tail sticking out.) Using your index finger, middle finger, and thumb as a guide, press the sides. Turn the ball and repeat a couple more times to give the onigiri three corners and three flat sides; it will be about 1 in [2.5 cm] thick. Don't press too hard; the onigiri should be firm on the outside but soft and airy on the inside. Place the finished onigiri on the prepared plate. Repeat with the remaining ingredients.

Hold an onigiri in one hand and wrap a piece of nori around it like a robe, starting at the back of the triangle and ending in front. Press gently to fix the nori in place. Repeat with the remaining onigiri and nori. Sprinkle with the furikake (if using).

Eat immediately.

MAKES 6 TRIANGULAR ONIGIRI

GRILLED
CRAB CAKE ONIGIRI

Unlike the Western crab cake, this version is made with rice as a base. Instead of bread crumbs, mayonnaise, and spices, I use miso paste, a seasoning made with fermented rice (*koji*), soybeans, wheat or other grains, and salt. Since all miso pastes are salty, don't use any salt when cooking the rice or molding the onigiri. If you can't find shimeji mushrooms, substitute any fresh mushroom of your choice.

1½ cups [330 g] uncooked short- or medium-grain white or haiga rice

1¾ cups [420 ml] filtered water

2 Tbsp sake

1 Tbsp soy sauce

One 2-in [5-cm] square konbu seaweed

5 oz [140 g] Dungeness crabmeat or other crabmeat, flaked

3 oz [85 g] shimeji brown mushrooms, trimmed and separated

¼ cup [10 g] chopped fresh chives

2 Tbsp freshly grated lemon zest

MISO SAUCE
¼ cup [65 g] red or white miso paste

2 Tbsp mirin

2 tsp soy sauce

1 tsp cane sugar

1 Tbsp sesame oil or melted butter

3 Tbsp sesame seeds, toasted (see page 27; optional)

cont'd

Place the rice in a medium bowl and rinse under cool running water, using your hands to gently swish the grains for about 10 seconds. Drain completely.

Pour the filtered water into a heavy-bottomed pot with a tight-fitting lid. Add the rice and let soak for about 30 minutes.

Add the sake and soy sauce to the rice and stir until combined. Top the rice with the konbu, crabmeat, and mushrooms.

Place the pot, uncovered, over medium heat and bring to a boil. The water should bubble around the rim evenly. Cover the pot, turn the heat to very low,

and cook, without peeking, for 20 minutes. Remove from the heat and, without opening the lid, let stand for 15 minutes.

Uncover the pot and gently fluff the rice with a rice paddle or wooden spoon, incorporating the crab and mushrooms. Re-cover and let stand for 5 minutes more. Remove the konbu (enjoy it as a snack). When cool enough to handle, the rice mixture is ready to make onigiri.

Have ready a large plate or cutting board to hold the finished onigiri. Prepare a small bowl of water for wetting your hands. Arrange near the plate.

Add half of the chives and the lemon zest to the rice and toss gently, without mashing the grains.

Divide the rice into six equal portions. Scoop one portion into a small teacup or bowl.

Moisten your hands with the water to keep the rice from sticking to them.

Gently tap the teacup or bowl to loosen the rice into your palm. Cup one hand to hold the rice ball. Press gently with your other hand, cupping your hand around the rice, to create one corner of the triangular shape. Using your index finger, middle finger, and thumb as a guide, press the sides. Turn the ball and repeat a couple more times to give the onigiri three corners and three flat sides; it will be about 1 in [2.5 cm] thick. Don't press too hard; the onigiri should be firm on the outside but soft and airy on the inside. Place the finished onigiri on the prepared plate. Repeat with the remaining ingredients.

To make the miso sauce
In a small bowl, whisk together the miso paste, mirin, soy sauce, and sugar. Set aside.

Prepare a charcoal grill, set a gas grill to medium, place a grill pan over medium-high heat, or position an oven rack 6 in [15 cm] from the heat source and preheat the broiler. Line a baking sheet (if using) with aluminum foil.

Place the miso sauce in a small bowl next to the grill.

Brush the onigiri on both sides with sesame oil to prevent them from sticking to the grill.

Grill the onigiri until crisp and lightly toasted, 4 to 5 minutes per side, depending on the heat. While grilling, baste with the miso sauce a few times; the sauce should be absorbed and the onigiri should not be moist. (Be careful, as the onigiri can burn.) Sprinkle with the sesame seeds (if using) and remaining chives.

Eat immediately.

MAKES 6 TRIANGULAR ONIGIRI

SALMON AND DILL ONIGIRI

This is the easiest way to make a totally satisfying and easy seafood onigiri. You can make this onigiri with smoked salmon or leftover grilled salmon. Lemon adds a lovely fragrance, but I sometimes use yuzu, a beautiful Japanese citrus. If you live in California, that's the citrus tree to plant.

1 Tbsp canola oil (if using smoked salmon)

6 oz [170 g] smoked salmon or grilled salmon, thinly sliced

2 sheets nori

2 tsp sea salt

3 Tbsp chopped fresh dill, plus a few sprigs for garnish

1 tsp freshly grated yuzu or lemon zest

1 recipe White Rice or Haiga Rice (page 18), Brown Rice (page 20), or Multigrain Rice (page 24)

3 Tbsp Sesame Furikake (page 30) or Kale Furikake (page 28)

If using smoked salmon, in a medium skillet over medium heat, warm the canola oil. Add the smoked salmon and cook until

opaque, about 15 seconds per side. Remove the salmon from the skillet.

If using grilled salmon, remove the skin and bones, if any. Flake the meat with your hands, then chop coarsely. Set aside.

Cut each nori sheet lengthwise into three strips; these are for wrapping the onigiri. Set aside in a dry place.

Have ready a large plate or cutting board to hold the finished onigiri. Prepare

cont'd

a small bowl of water for wetting your hands and a small bowl containing the salt. Arrange near the plate.

Fold the salmon, dill, and yuzu zest into the rice, combining gently, without mashing the grains.

Divide the rice into six equal portions. Scoop one portion into a small teacup or bowl.

Moisten your hands with the water to keep the rice from sticking to them. Lightly dip the tips of the index, middle, and ring fingers of one hand into the bowl of water, then into the bowl of salt. Rub the

salt onto your palms. You should have a light coating on your palms.

Gently tap the teacup or bowl to loosen the rice into your palm. Cup one hand to hold the rice ball. Press gently with your other hand, cupping your hand around the rice, to create one corner of the triangular shape. Using your index finger, middle finger, and thumb as a guide, press the sides. Turn the ball and repeat a couple more times to give the onigiri three corners and three flat sides; it will be about 1 in [2.5 cm] thick. Don't press too hard; the onigiri should

be firm on the outside but soft and airy on the inside. Place the finished onigiri on the prepared plate. Repeat with the remaining ingredients.

Hold an onigiri in one hand and wrap a piece of nori around the edge of the triangle. Press gently to fix the nori in place. Repeat with the remaining onigiri and nori. Sprinkle with the furikake and garnish with dill sprigs.

Eat immediately.

MAKES 6 TRIANGULAR ONIGIRI

TUNA MELT ONIGIRI

When my family moved to Los Angeles, my parents took us out to Bob's Big Boy, where I had a tuna melt sandwich for the first time. Here is the onigiri version of a tuna melt. This actually makes sense, as the combination of tuna and mayonnaise is a very popular onigiri filling. This is one onigiri you'll want to eat with a fork and knife.

One 6-oz [170-g] can water-packed white meat tuna, drained

1 Tbsp minced celery

1 Tbsp minced red onion

½ tsp minced fresh parsley

⅓ cup [80 g] mayonnaise

1 tsp mustard

Freshly ground black pepper

2 tsp sea salt

1 recipe White Rice or Haiga Rice (page 18), Brown Rice (page 20), or Multigrain Rice (page 24)

1 Tbsp melted butter

6 Tbsp [30 g] shredded medium-sharp Cheddar cheese

Minced fresh chives for garnish

In a small bowl, break up the tuna with a fork. Stir in the celery, onion, and parsley to combine, followed by the mayonnaise and mustard. Season with pepper.

Have ready a large plate or cutting board to hold the finished onigiri. Prepare a small bowl of water for wetting your hands and a small bowl containing the salt. Arrange near the plate.

Divide the rice into six equal portions. Scoop one portion into a small teacup or bowl.

cont'd

Moisten your hands with the water to keep the rice from sticking to them. Lightly dip the tips of the index, middle, and ring fingers of one hand into the bowl of water, then into the bowl of salt. Rub the salt onto your palms. You should have a light coating on your palms.

Gently tap the teacup or bowl to loosen the rice into your palm. Cup one hand to hold the rice ball. Press gently with your other hand, cupping your hand around the rice, to create one corner of the triangular shape. Using your index finger, middle finger, and thumb as a guide, press the sides. Turn the ball

and repeat a couple more times to give the onigiri three corners and three flat sides; it will be about 1 in [2.5 cm] thick. Don't press too hard; the onigiri should be firm on the outside but soft and airy on the inside. Place the finished onigiri on the prepared plate. Repeat with the remaining ingredients.

Position an oven rack about 6 in [15 cm] from the heat source and preheat the broiler. Line a baking sheet with aluminum foil.

Brush the onigiri on both sides with melted butter and place them on the baking sheet.

Broil the onigiri until toasted but not burnt, 3 to 4 minutes per side. Remove from the broiler and spread the top of each onigiri with 1 Tbsp of the tuna filling. Return to the broiler for 1 minute, then sprinkle the onigiri with 1 Tbsp of the cheese. Place the baking sheet under the broiler once again and broil until the cheese has melted, about 1 minute more. Garnish with chives.

Eat immediately.

MAKES 6 TRIANGULAR ONIGIRI

SMOKED TROUT ONIGIRI
WITH LEMON

Trout is a mild freshwater fish that is especially delicious when smoked. You can make fancy smoked trout onigiri balls using plastic wrap as a guide for molding. You will instantly be elevated to sushi master if you serve this easy-to-assemble onigiri at your next party.

¼ cup [60 ml] Sushi Vinegar (page 119)

1 recipe White Rice or Haiga Rice (page 18)

3 Tbsp minced peeled fresh ginger

12 fresh shiso leaves; 8 leaves finely chopped, 4 leaves minced

3 Tbsp white sesame seeds, toasted (see page 27)

6 oz [170 g] smoked trout

2 slices lemon, cut into 12 wedges

Pickled Young Ginger (page 118) for serving

Have ready a large plate or cutting board to hold the finished onigiri. Prepare a small bowl of water for wetting your hands. Arrange near the plate.

Cut out a large piece of plastic wrap and drape over a small teacup or bowl.

Add the sushi vinegar to the rice and toss gently, without mashing the grains. Then, fold the ginger, finely chopped shiso, and sesame seeds into the rice, combining gently.

Divide the rice and smoked trout each into twelve equal portions. Scoop one portion of the rice into the plastic-lined teacup or bowl. Using your fingers (it doesn't matter which fingers are used here), press an indentation into the rice. Place one portion of the trout into the indentation and mold the rice around it.

Moisten your hands with the water to keep the rice from sticking to them.

Gather the plastic wrap and lift the onigiri out of the teacup with your hands. Twist the ends of the plastic wrap and mold the rice into a ball. Unwrap the plastic, remove the onigiri, and give it a gentle final press with your slightly wet hands. Don't press too hard; the onigiri should be firm on the outside but soft and airy on the inside. Place the finished onigiri on the prepared plate. Repeat with the remaining ingredients.

Garnish with the lemon wedges and sprinkle with the minced shiso.

Eat immediately, served with pickled ginger.

MAKES 12 BALL ONIGIRI

AMAKARA
CHICKEN ONIGIRI

If you like yakitori (grilled chicken), you'll know this sauce. Add chili pepper to make this spicier, or mayonnaise to make it richer in umami.

1 Tbsp sake

1 Tbsp mirin

1 Tbsp soy sauce

½ tsp cane sugar

½ garlic clove, grated

1 oz [30 g] minced peeled fresh ginger

6 oz [170 g] skin-on boneless chicken thighs

2 sheets nori (optional)

2 tsp sea salt

½ cup [20 g] chopped fresh chives

1 recipe White Rice or Haiga Rice (page 18), Brown Rice (page 20), or Multigrain Rice (page 24)

3 Tbsp Sesame Furikake (page 30)

Freshly ground black pepper

Position an oven rack about 6 in [15 cm] from the heat source and preheat the broiler. Line a baking sheet with aluminum foil.

In a small bowl, stir together the sake, mirin, soy sauce, sugar, garlic, and ginger. Place the sauce near the broiler.

Place the chicken skin-side down on a work surface. Make four or five slits crosswise on the meat, about ¼ in [6 mm] deep. Arrange the chicken skin-side down on the prepared baking sheet.

cont'd

Broil the chicken until it starts to brown, 4 to 5 minutes. Brush the chicken with the sauce, repeating on the same side three times every 2 minutes, until toasted. Flip the chicken and baste the skin with the sauce three or four times, until the skin gets nicely toasted, about 5 minutes. Remove from the heat and let rest for 5 minutes. Cut the chicken into ⅜-in [1-cm] dice. Set aside. (The chicken will keep for 2 days in the refrigerator. Bring to room temperature before using.)

If wrapping the onigiri, cut each nori sheet lengthwise into three strips. Set aside in a dry place.

Have ready a large plate or cutting board to hold the finished onigiri. Prepare a small bowl of water for wetting your hands and a small bowl containing the salt. Arrange near the plate.

Fold the chicken and chives into the rice, combining gently, without mashing the grains.

Divide the rice into six equal portions. Scoop one portion into a small teacup or bowl.

Moisten your hands with the water to keep the rice from sticking to them. Lightly dip the tips of the index, middle, and ring fingers of one hand into the bowl of water, then

into the bowl of salt. Rub the salt onto your palms. You should have a light coating on your palms.

Gently tap the teacup or bowl to loosen the rice into your palm. Cup one hand to hold the rice ball. Press gently with your other hand, cupping your hand around the rice, to create one corner of the triangular shape. Using your index finger, middle finger, and thumb as a guide, press the sides. Turn the ball and repeat a couple more times to give the onigiri three corners and three flat sides; it will be about 1 in [2.5 cm] thick. Don't press too hard; the onigiri should be firm on the outside but soft and airy on the inside. Place the finished onigiri on the prepared plate. Repeat with the remaining ingredients.

Hold an onigiri in one hand and wrap a piece of nori around it like a robe, starting at the back of the triangle and ending in front. Press gently to fix the nori in place. Repeat with the remaining onigiri and nori. Sprinkle with the furikake and pepper.

Eat immediately.

MAKES 6 TRIANGULAR ONIGIRI

TATSUTA
FRIED CHICKEN ONIGIRI

These chicken bites soak in a soy-ginger marinade before they are fried in hot oil. The name Tatsuta comes from the Tatsuta River in Nara Prefecture, known for its crimson autumn leaves, which the crispy reddish-brown chicken is said to resemble.

1 Tbsp sesame oil

1 Tbsp fresh lemon juice

2 tsp soy sauce

2 tsp sake

2 tsp mirin

½ tsp cane sugar

1 green onion, both white and green parts, chopped

2 tsp grated peeled fresh ginger

6 oz [170 g] skin-on boneless chicken thighs, cut into 1½-in [4-cm] cubes

2 Tbsp cornstarch

Canola, peanut, or rice bran oil for frying

2 sheets nori

2 tsp sea salt

1 recipe White Rice or Haiga Rice (page 18), Brown Rice (page 20), or Multigrain Rice (page 24)

3 Tbsp Sesame Furikake (page 30)

Shichimi togarashi pepper for serving

In a large bowl, stir together the sesame oil, lemon juice, soy sauce, sake, mirin, sugar, green onion, and ginger. Add the chicken, turn to coat, and let marinate for 30 to 60 minutes.

Transfer the chicken to a colander and let the marinade drain away. Discard the marinade.

Place the cornstarch in a shallow bowl. Dredge the chicken in the cornstarch and dust off the excess.

Pour enough canola oil into a 2-qt [2-L] cast-iron Dutch oven to come up halfway up the sides. Heat over medium-high heat until an instant-read thermometer reads 350°F [180°C]. Set a wire rack over a baking sheet.

Working in batches, gently drop four or five chicken pieces into the hot oil. Fry on all sides until golden brown, 4 to 5 minutes. Remove with a slotted spoon and drain on the prepared rack. Repeat until all the chicken is fried, checking the oil temperature before frying each batch. Let cool, then cut the chicken pieces in half and set aside.

Cut each nori sheet crosswise into three strips; these are for wrapping the onigiri. Set aside in a dry place.

Have ready a large plate or cutting board to hold the finished onigiri. Prepare a small bowl of water for wetting your hands, a small bowl containing the salt, and a bowl containing the chicken. Blot out excess oil on the chicken with a paper towel. Arrange near the plate.

Divide the rice into six equal portions. Scoop one portion into a small teacup or bowl. Using your fingers (it doesn't matter which fingers are used here), press an indentation into the rice. Add one-sixth of the chicken filling into the indentation and mold the rice around it.

Moisten your hands with the water to keep the rice from sticking to them. Lightly dip the tips of the index, middle, and ring fingers of one hand into the bowl of water, then into the bowl of salt. Rub the salt onto your palms. You should have a light coating on your palms.

cont'd

Gently tap the teacup or bowl to loosen the rice into your palm. Cup one hand to hold the rice ball. Press gently with your other hand, cupping your hand around the rice, to create one corner of the triangular shape. Using your index finger, middle finger, and thumb as a guide, press the sides. Turn the ball and repeat a couple more times to give the onigiri three corners and three flat sides; it will be about 1 in [2.5 cm] thick. Don't press too hard; the onigiri should be firm on the outside but soft and airy on the inside. Place the finished onigiri on the prepared plate. Repeat with the remaining ingredients.

Hold an onigiri in one hand and wrap a piece of nori around it like a robe, starting at the back of the triangle and ending in front. Press gently to fix the nori in place. Repeat with the remaining onigiri and nori. Sprinkle with the furikake and shichimi pepper.

Eat immediately.

MAKES 6 TRIANGULAR ONIGIRI

MISO CON CARNE ONIGIRI

The minced ginger, green onion, and chile pepper in this sauce make it spicy. You can sub in ground chicken or beef for the pork, and the filling keeps, refrigerated, for up to 3 days.

1 Tbsp red miso paste

1 tsp cane sugar

1 Tbsp mirin

2 tsp soy sauce

1 green onion, both white and green parts, minced

1 Tbsp minced peeled fresh ginger

½ garlic clove, minced

1 Japanese dried red chile, seeded and minced

¼ tsp freshly ground black pepper

1 Tbsp sesame oil

6 oz [170 g] ground pork

2 sheets nori

2 tsp sea salt

¼ cup [10 g] chopped fresh chives

1 recipe White Rice or Haiga Rice (page 18), Brown Rice (page 20), or Multigrain Rice (page 24)

3 Tbsp Sesame Furikake (page 30)

In a small bowl, whisk together the miso, sugar, mirin, and soy sauce. Stir in the green onion, ginger, garlic, dried chile, and black pepper. Set aside.

In a medium skillet over medium heat, warm the sesame oil. Add the pork and cook until it is brown and crumbly, stirring often with a wooden spoon and breaking up the lumps, about 5 minutes. Stir in the miso sauce, turn the heat to low, and cook until the pork has absorbed the

cont'd

liquid, about 5 minutes more. Remove from the heat and let cool.

Cut each nori sheet crosswise into three strips; these are for wrapping the onigiri. Set aside in a dry place.

Have ready a large plate or cutting board to hold the finished onigiri. Prepare a small bowl of water for wetting your hands, a small bowl containing the salt, and a bowl containing the pork. Arrange near the plate.

Fold the chives into the rice, combining gently, without mashing the grains.

Divide the rice into six equal portions. Scoop one portion into a small teacup or bowl. Using your fingers (it doesn't matter which fingers are used here), press an indentation into the rice. Add 1 Tbsp of the pork into the indentation and mold the rice around it. (You will have some leftover pork; enjoy it later.)

Moisten your hands with the water to keep the rice from sticking to them. Lightly dip the tips of the index, middle, and ring fingers of one hand into the bowl of water, then into the bowl of salt. Rub the salt onto your palms. You should have a light coating on your palms.

Gently tap the teacup or bowl to loosen the rice into your palm. Cup one hand to hold the rice ball. Press gently with your other hand, cupping your hand around the rice, to create one corner of the triangular shape. Using your index finger, middle finger, and thumb as a guide, press the sides. Turn the ball and repeat a couple more times to give the onigiri three corners and three flat sides; it will be about 1 in [2.5 cm] thick. Don't press too hard; the onigiri should be firm on the outside but soft and airy on the inside. Place the finished onigiri on the prepared plate. Repeat with the remaining ingredients.

cont'd

Hold an onigiri in one hand and wrap a piece of nori around it like a robe, starting at the back of the triangle and ending in front. Press gently to fix the nori in place. Repeat with the remaining onigiri and nori. Sprinkle with the furikake.

Eat immediately.

MAKES 6 TRIANGULAR ONIGIRI

PANFRIED
PORK ONIGIRI

My grandmother had a plum tree in her garden that was as old as she was. Every year she made umeboshi using its sour plums. Grandmother would soak the plums in a brine with red shiso leaves and leave them in the sun to dry. When I visited her in Kamakura, she would send me back to the United States with jars of her umeboshi. When she celebrated her 100th birthday, I cooked an umeboshi-themed dinner for her. The pork loin was one of the dishes we did on the grill.

4 oz [115 g] umeboshi

1½ cups [360 ml] filtered water

2 tsp cane sugar

⅓ cup [80 ml] sake

2 tsp mirin

2 tsp soy sauce

1 oz [30 g] grated peeled fresh ginger

1 tsp vegetable oil

8 oz [230 g] boneless pork loin, trimmed and cut crosswise into ½-in [12-mm] slices

Sea salt

1 green onion, both white and green parts, minced

4 fresh shiso leaves, minced

2 sheets nori

1 recipe White Rice or Haiga Rice (page 18), Brown Rice (page 20), or Multigrain Rice (page 24)

3 Tbsp Sesame Furikake (page 30)

In a small saucepan, combine the umeboshi and water. Bring to a simmer over low heat and cook for 10 minutes. Drain and let cool.

cont'd

In a small bowl, mash the umeboshi with the back of a spoon. Discard the pits. Stir in the sugar, sake, mirin, soy sauce, and ginger. Transfer the umeboshi mixture to a food processor and purée until smooth. Return the purée to the same small saucepan and simmer over low heat until thickened, 3 to 4 minutes. Let cool, transfer to a small bowl, and set aside.

In a medium frying pan over medium heat, warm the vegetable oil. Season the pork with salt and add to the pan. Fry the pork until brown, 2 to 3 minutes per side. It can be slightly pink and juicy inside. Transfer to a cutting board and let cool. Cut the pork into ½-in [12-mm] cubes and put in a small bowl. Add 2 Tbsp of the umeboshi sauce, the green onion, and shiso and stir until combined. Reserve the remaining umeboshi sauce for dipping.

Cut each nori sheet crosswise into three strips; these are for wrapping the onigiri. Set aside in a dry place.

Have ready a large plate or cutting board to hold the finished onigiri. Prepare a small bowl of water for wetting your hands, a small bowl containing 2 tsp salt, and the bowl containing the pork. Arrange near the plate.

Divide the rice into six equal portions. Scoop one portion into a small teacup or bowl. Using your fingers (it doesn't matter which fingers are used here), press an indentation into the rice. Add one-sixth of the pork into the indentation and mold the rice around it.

Moisten your hands with the water to keep the rice from sticking to them. Lightly dip the tips of the index, middle, and ring fingers of one hand into the bowl of water, then into the bowl of salt. Rub the salt onto your palms. You should have a light coating on your palms.

Gently tap the teacup or bowl to loosen the rice into your palm. Cup one hand to hold the rice ball. Press gently with your other hand, cupping your hand around the rice, to create one corner of the triangular shape. Using your index finger, middle finger, and thumb as a guide, press the sides. Turn the ball and repeat a couple more times to give the onigiri three corners and three flat sides; it will be about 1 in [2.5 cm] thick. Don't press too hard; the onigiri should be firm on the outside but soft and airy on the inside. Place the finished onigiri on the prepared plate. Repeat with the remaining ingredients.

Hold an onigiri in one hand and wrap a piece of nori around it like a robe, starting at the back of the triangle and ending in front. Press gently to fix the nori in place. Repeat with the remaining onigiri and nori. Sprinkle with the furikake.

Eat immediately, passing any remaining umeboshi sauce at the table for dipping.

MAKES 6 TRIANGULAR ONIGIRI

BACON AND SCRAMBLED EGG ONIGIRI

This onigiri is a little fatty from the eggs scrambled in butter and the bacon. If you like, you can hold it all together by wrapping it like an envelope (see page 33).

3 eggs

2¼ tsp sea salt

¼ tsp freshly ground black pepper

1 Tbsp butter

1 green onion; white parts chopped, green parts thinly sliced

1 recipe White Rice or Haiga Rice (page 18), Brown Rice (page 20), or Multigrain Rice (page 24)

6 oz [170 g] cooked bacon, cut into ⅛-in (4-mm) slices

In a medium bowl, beat together the eggs, ¼ tsp of the salt, and the pepper.

In a nonstick or cast-iron frying pan over medium-low heat, melt the butter. Pour in the eggs and cook, stirring with a spatula, until soft lumps of eggs begin to form, about 30 seconds.

Sprinkle the chopped green onion across the eggs, turn the heat to low, and shift from stirring to folding the lumps. As soon as the egg sets, about 1 minute, remove from the heat and transfer to a plate.

Have ready a large plate or cutting board to hold the finished onigiri. Prepare a small bowl of water for wetting your hands and small bowl containing the remaining 2 tsp salt. Arrange near the plate.

cont'd

Cut out a large piece of plastic wrap and drape over a small teacup or bowl.

Fold the scrambled eggs into the rice, combining gently, without mashing the grains.

Divide the rice into twelve equal portions. Scoop one portion of the rice into the plastic-lined teacup or bowl.

Moisten your hands with the water to keep the rice from sticking to them. Lightly dip the tips of the index, middle, and ring fingers of one hand into the bowl of water, then into the bowl of salt. Rub the salt onto your palms. You should have a light coating on your palms.

Gather the plastic wrap and lift the onigiri out of the teacup with your hands. Twist the ends of the plastic wrap and mold the rice into a ball. Unwrap the plastic, remove the onigiri, and give it a gentle final press with your slightly wet hands. Don't press too hard; the onigiri should be firm on the outside but soft and airy on the inside. Place the finished onigiri on the prepared plate. Top with a slice of bacon. Repeat with the remaining ingredients. Garnish with the sliced green onion.

Eat immediately.

MAKES 12 BALL ONIGIRI

SUKIYAKI ONIGIRI

This onigiri is inspired by sukiyaki, a hot pot dish of thinly sliced beef cooked with tofu and vegetables. You can find this cut of beef at Japanese markets, or simulate it by asking a butcher to cut a well-marbled beef sirloin very thinly.

1 Tbsp vegetable oil

½ medium onion, chopped

8 oz [230 g] beef sirloin, very thinly sliced

2 Tbsp sake

2 Tbsp soy sauce

1 Tbsp mirin

1 tsp cane sugar

1 Tbsp minced peeled fresh ginger

3 sheets nori (optional)

2 tsp sea salt

1 recipe White Rice or Haiga Rice (page 18) or Brown Rice (page 20)

2 Tbsp Sesame Furikake (page 30)

In a medium skillet over medium heat, warm the vegetable oil. Add the onion and sauté until softened, about 2 minutes. Add the beef and cook until medium-rare, about 30 seconds per side. Turn the heat to low and stir in the sake, soy sauce, mirin, sugar, and ginger. Cook until the beef has absorbed the liquid, 1 to 2 minutes. Remove from the heat, let cool, and cut the sukiyaki into ½-in [12-mm] pieces.

If wrapping the onigiri, cut each nori sheet at a diagonal into two sheets. Set aside in a dry place.

cont'd

Have ready a large plate or cutting board to hold the finished onigiri. Prepare a small bowl of water for wetting your hands, a small bowl containing the salt, and a bowl containing the sukiyaki. Blot out excess liquid in the sukiyaki with a paper towel. Arrange near the plate.

Divide the rice into six equal portions. Scoop one portion into a small teacup or bowl. Using your fingers (it doesn't matter which fingers are used here), press an indentation into the rice. Add 1½ Tbsp of the sukiyaki into the indentation and mold the rice around it.

Moisten your hands with the water to keep the rice from sticking to them. Lightly dip the tips of the index, middle, and ring fingers of one hand into the bowl of water, then into the bowl of salt. Rub the salt onto your palms. You should have a light coating on your palms.

Gently tap the teacup or bowl to loosen the rice into your palm. Cup one hand to hold the rice ball. Press gently with your other hand, cupping your hand around the rice, to create one corner of the triangular shape. Using your index finger, middle finger, and thumb as a guide, press the sides. Turn the ball

and repeat a couple more times to give the onigiri three corners and three flat sides; it will be about 1 in [2.5 cm] thick. Don't press too hard; the onigiri should be firm on the outside but soft and airy on the inside. Place the finished onigiri on the prepared plate. Repeat with the remaining ingredients.

Hold an onigiri in one hand and wrap a piece of nori around it so the entire ball is wrapped. Press gently to fix the nori in place. Repeat with the remaining onigiri and nori. Sprinkle with the furikake.

Eat immediately.

MAKES 6 TRIANGULAR ONIGIRI

INARi SUSHi
"FOOTBALLS"

The word *inari* comes from the Japanese deity known for protecting rice, agriculture, and fertility. Inari and her attendant foxlike creatures are said to have a soft spot for fried tofu. Some Japanese Americans call these tofu pouches "footballs," which makes me smile. Sold in the tofu or frozen section of Japanese markets, they come in square and rectangular shapes. If you get the rectangular ones, you will need to cut them in half to make a square.

4 cups [960 ml] filtered water

5 fried tofu pouches (*abura-age*), 2¾ by 5½ in [7 by 14 cm], or 10 fried tofu pouches (*abura-age*), 2¾ by 2¾ in [7 by 7 cm]

One 4-in [10-cm] piece konbu seaweed

3 Tbsp soy sauce

2 Tbsp mirin

1 Tbsp cane sugar

5 Tbsp Sushi Vinegar (page 119)

3 Tbsp white or black sesame seeds, toasted (see page 27)

1 recipe White Rice or Haiga Rice (page 18), Brown Rice (page 20), or Multigrain Rice (page 24)

1 Japanese or Persian cucumber, cut into ¼-in [6-mm] slices (optional)

2 Tbsp Pickled Young Ginger (page 118; optional)

2 Tbsp Sesame Furikake (page 30) or Kale Furikake (page 28)

In a medium saucepan over medium heat, combine 2 cups [480 ml] of the water and the tofu pouches and bring to a boil. Cook for

cont'd

2 minutes to remove excess oil from the pouches, then drain and let cool. Gently squeeze the water from the pouches.

In the same saucepan over medium heat, warm the remaining 2 cups [480 ml] water and the konbu. Remove the konbu (enjoy it as a snack) just before the water comes to a boil.

Add the soy sauce, mirin, sugar, and blanched tofu pouches to the saucepan and simmer for 20 minutes. Remove from the heat and let the pouches soak in the liquid for about 15 minutes.

If using the 2¾-by-5½-in [7-by-14-cm] tofu pouches, cut them crosswise in half to make an opening. You

should have ten square pouches, each measuring approximately 2¾ by 2¾ in [7 by 7 cm], with an opening on one end like a pillowcase.

Gently squeeze the liquid from the seasoned tofu pouches. They should still feel moist. Transfer to a bowl.

Have ready a large plate or cutting board to hold the finished inari sushi. Prepare a small bowl of water for wetting your hands and the bowl containing the tofu pouches. Arrange near the plate.

Add the vinegar and sesame seeds to the rice and toss gently, without mashing the grains.

Divide the rice into ten equal portions. Scoop one portion into a small teacup or bowl.

Moisten your hands with the water to keep the rice from sticking to them.

Gently tap the teacup or bowl to loosen the rice into your palm. Press gently into your palm, then use the index finger, middle finger, and thumb of your other hand to gently press the two ends of the ball to form a log. Don't press too hard; the onigiri should be firm on the outside but soft and airy on the inside. Place the finished onigiri on the prepared plate. Repeat with the remaining ingredients.

Gently open a tofu pouch, without tearing it. Stuff the pouch with an onigiri. Fold the end of the pouch under to seal the opening. Alternatively, you can fold over about ½ in [12 mm] of the pouch to create a wider opening and arrange three cucumber slices (if using) in each pouch. Sprinkle with the furikake.

Eat immediately.

MAKES 10 INARI SUSHI

EVERYDAY
MISO SOUP

Just as onigiri can be served at any meal, miso soup—though traditionally a breakfast soup—can be too. And it is just as much a blank canvas. I use turnips here, but you can add other seasonal vegetables, meat, or seafood. If you are vegetarian, you can skip the bonito flakes used to make the dashi and use just the konbu. Miso comes in a variety of flavors and textures. White miso is milder and sweeter and tends to contain more *koji* (fermented rice). Red miso is salty and savory. Try mixing a couple of varieties to create your favorite miso blend.

DASHI
One 2-in [5-cm] piece konbu seaweed

4½ cups [1 L] filtered water

1 oz [30 g] bonito flakes

¼ cup [70 g] miso (red, white, or any type of miso you like)

3 to 5 baby turnips, cut crosswise into ¼-in [6-mm] slices

8 oz [230 g] soft or firm tofu, drained

2 green onions, both white and green parts, cut crosswise into ⅛-in [4-mm] slices

To make the dashi
Take the konbu and, using scissors, cut several crosswise slits into it.

In a medium saucepan over high heat, combine the water and konbu and bring to a boil. Just before the water comes to a full boil, pluck out the konbu. (Discard or set aside to reuse.) Turn the heat to low and add the bonito flakes. Let the bonito flakes steep in the dashi for a couple of minutes, then turn off the heat. Strain the dashi in a sieve lined with a paper towel or cheesecloth. (Discard the bonito flakes or set aside to reuse.)

In a small bowl, dissolve the miso with ¼ cup [60 ml] of the dashi. Set aside.

In a medium saucepan over medium heat, combine the remaining dashi and the turnips. Bring to a boil, then turn the heat to low

and add the tofu and the miso mixture. Stir once. (Taste and, if the soup tastes weak, add more miso; if the soup tastes salty, adjust with dashi or water.) Remove from the heat.

Divide the miso soup among four bowls and garnish with the green onions.

Eat immediately.

SERVES 4

NOTE: To make more dashi from the used konbu and bonito, combine them in a medium saucepan with 4½ cups [1 L] filtered water. Bring to a boil over high heat, then turn the heat to low and simmer for 5 minutes. Set a fine-mesh strainer lined with a paper towel or cheesecloth over a bowl and pour the dashi through it. Discard the solids. Store in an airtight container in the refrigerator for up to 3 days.

CRISPY ONIGIRI
TEA SOUP

You can use any onigiri to make this soup, or substitute chicken broth, miso soup, or dashi (see page 108) for the green tea. To eat, break up the onigiri with chopsticks or a spoon and spread the rice in the soup.

6 umeboshi

2 Tbsp minced peeled fresh ginger

6 fresh shiso leaves, minced

1 sheet nori (optional)

1 recipe White Rice or Haiga Rice (page 18), Brown Rice (page 20), or Multigrain Rice (page 24)

1 Tbsp sesame oil

2 Tbsp soy sauce

6 cups [1.4 L] filtered water

2 Tbsp loose-leaf green tea

2 Tbsp sesame seeds, toasted (see page 27)

2 Tbsp chopped fresh chives

1 Tbsp freshly grated lemon zest

In a small bowl, combine the umeboshi, ginger, and shiso.

If wrapping the onigiri, cut the nori crosswise into six strips. Set aside in a dry place.

Have ready a large plate or cutting board to hold the finished onigiri. Prepare a small bowl of water for wetting your hands. Arrange near the plate.

Fold the umeboshi mixture into the rice, combining gently, without mashing the grains. Divide the rice into six equal portions. Scoop one portion into a small teacup or bowl.

cont'd

111

Moisten your hands with the water to keep the rice from sticking to them. Lightly dip the tips of the index, middle, and ring fingers of one hand into the bowl of water.

Gently tap the teacup or bowl to loosen the rice into your palm. Press gently into your palm, then use the index finger, middle finger, and thumb of your other hand to gently press the two ends of the ball to form a log, about 1½ in [4 cm] wide and 2½ in [6 cm] long. Don't press too hard; the onigiri should be firm on the outside but soft and airy on the inside. Place the finished onigiri on the prepared plate. Repeat with the remaining ingredients.

Position an oven rack about 6 in [15 cm] from the heat source and preheat the broiler. Line a baking sheet with aluminum foil.

Put the sesame oil in a small bowl and the soy sauce in another bowl and place near the broiler.

Brush the onigiri on both sides with sesame oil and place on the prepared baking sheet. Brush the tops of the onigiri with soy sauce.

Broil the onigiri until toasted, 3 to 4 minutes. Remove from the broiler, flip the onigiri, and brush the other side with the remaining soy sauce. Broil until the second side is toasted, 3 to 4 minutes more.

Bring the water to a boil, then let stand for 2 minutes. Pour into a teapot with the tea leaves and let steep for 1 minute.

Hold an onigiri in one hand and wrap a piece of nori around it like a belt, starting at the center and wrapping around the log. Press gently to fix the nori in place. Repeat with the remaining onigiri and nori.

Divide the onigiri among six soup bowls and pour 1 cup [240 ml] of the hot tea over each. Garnish with the sesame seeds, chives, and lemon zest.

Eat immediately.

SERVES 6

ONIGIRI
EGGS

This is the soft-boiled egg you'll find in ramen or other Japanese noodle soups. Used as an onigiri filling, it looks like a Scotch egg, but instead of a hard-boiled egg wrapped in sausage meat, the marinated soft-boiled egg is wrapped in rice and nori. Use a chicken egg for a big onigiri and a quail egg for a small onigiri. These marinated eggs are easy to make and can also be used as a side in a bento box.

DIPPING SAUCE

1½ cups [360 ml] dashi (see page 108)

¼ cup [60 ml] soy sauce

¼ cup [60 ml] mirin

6 chicken eggs or 12 quail eggs

To make the dipping sauce

In a medium saucepan over low heat, combine the dashi, soy sauce, and mirin, and cook for a couple of minutes. Remove from the heat and let cool to room temperature.

Prepare a large bowl of ice water and place next to the stove top.

If using chicken eggs, in a medium saucepan over high heat, bring 2 qt (2 L) of water to a boil.

Pierce the end of each chicken egg with a thumb-tack to make a tiny hole, which will prevent the shells from cracking. Using a slotted spoon, lower the eggs into the water. Turn the heat to low and simmer

cont'd

for 6 minutes. As the eggs simmer, gently move them around in the pot with a wooden spoon, which will encourage the yolk to move to the center of the egg.

If using quail eggs, in a medium saucepan, combine 2 qt [2 L] water and the quail eggs (there is no need to pierce them), set over high heat, and bring to a boil. Turn the heat to low and simmer for 3 minutes.

With a slotted spoon, carefully transfer the eggs to the ice water and let cool for 3 minutes. Peel the eggs and put them in the dipping sauce. Let the eggs marinate in the refrigerator overnight, or up to 3 days.

MAKES 6 CHICKEN EGGS OR 12 QUAIL EGGS

SPICY
KiMPiRA ROOTS

Root vegetables are eaten for good luck in the New Year because their deep roots are a metaphor for personal grounding. "Kimpira style" describes a mixture of carrot and burdock that's julienned and sautéed in sake, soy, mirin, and red chiles.

1 tsp rice vinegar

1 medium carrot, peeled

6 oz [170 g] burdock root, scrubbed and hairy roots removed

2½ Tbsp sesame oil

3 Tbsp sake

1 Tbsp mirin

1 Tbsp soy sauce

1½ tsp cane sugar

½ Japanese dried red chile, seeded and minced

Sesame seeds for garnish

Fill a small bowl with cold water and add the rice vinegar. Cut the carrot and burdock into julienne that are about 2½ in [6 cm] long, putting them into the vinegar water to prevent any discoloration.

In a medium frying pan over medium heat, warm the sesame oil. Drain the carrot and burdock, add to the pan, and stir-fry for about 3 minutes. Add the sake and stir-fry about 2 minutes more. Add the mirin, soy sauce, and sugar and stir-fry until the burdock and carrot are cooked but still slightly al dente, 2 to 3 minutes. Stir in the red chile. Remove from the heat and let cool.

Garnish with sesame seeds before serving.

SERVES 2 TO 4

PiCKLED YOUNG GiNGER

Ginger is a refreshing accompaniment to just about any grilled meat, seafood, or vegetable dish. If you see young ginger at Asian markets or the farmers' market, make these pickles, which are quick and easy and not too sweet.

6 oz [170 g] young ginger

1½ oz [40 g] red beet (optional)

2 cups [480 ml] filtered water

1½ tsp sea salt

⅓ cup [60 g] cane sugar

1 cup [240 ml] rice vinegar

Peel the ginger and beet (if using) and cut into ⅟₁₆-in [2-mm] slices, using a mandoline, if you have one.

In a small saucepan over medium heat, bring 1 cup [240 ml] of the filtered water to a boil. Add the sliced ginger and beet, turn the heat to low, and cook for 10 seconds, then drain. Remove the beet and discard. While the ginger is still hot, toss with ½ tsp of the salt in a lidded container. Set aside.

In a medium saucepan over medium heat, combine the remaining 1 cup [240 ml] water, remaining 1 tsp salt, and the sugar and bring to a boil. Turn off the heat. Add the vinegar and stir a few times. Pour the hot vinegar marinade over the ginger. Marinate for at least 12 hours, or up to 48 hours, before eating.

Store in an airtight container in the refrigerator for up to 3 months.

MAKES ¾ CUP [90 G]

SUSHI VINEGAR

This is a seasoned vinegar recipe that is used for making sushi rice. Use 3 Tbsp for the White Rice or Haiga Rice (page 18), Brown Rice (page 20), or Multigrain Rice (page 24). You can also use it to make quick vegetable pickles (see page 117), by simply marinating the cut vegetables in the vinegar for an hour, or as the base for a dipping sauce for a chard wrap (see page 56).

¾ cup [180 ml] rice vinegar

¼ cup [55 g] cane sugar

1 Tbsp sea salt

In a small saucepan over low heat, combine the rice vinegar, sugar, and salt and cook, stirring, until the sugar dissolves. Let cool completely.

Store in an airtight container in a cool, dark place for up to 3 months.

MAKES ¾ CUP [180 ML]

INDEX

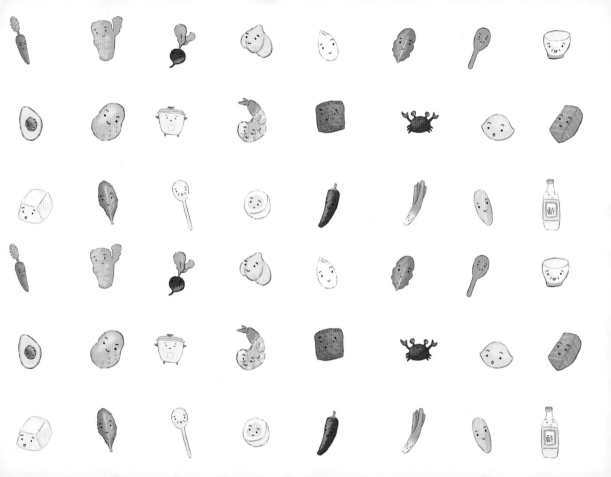